Antarctica Froze up Warmer

Illustrated Science Exploration by Rolf A. F. Witzsche

Antarctica Froze up Warmer

This book contains the transcript with images of the exploration video with the above title:
see: http://www.ice-age-ahead-iaa.ca/

Lead in:

Yes, the Earth was Radically Warmer when Antarctica froze up so long ago.

What does this mean? (A Special Exploration Project)

Antarctica froze up three quarters of the way of the climate collapse of the last 100 million years in Phanerozoic Climate history. Antarctica froze up roughly 32 million years ago when the Sun had cooled sufficiently for this to happen. Because the long-term climate collapse had unfolded in two overlaid cycles, Antarctica had thawed out again a few million years later as the Sun became warmer again for a period. After that, the Sun became colder again, so that Antarctica froze up once more and remained frozen thereafter, while the Sun continued to cool.

It would take another 10 million years, with the Sun getting still weaker and colder, for the Ice Age glaciation cycles to begin. We are presently 2 million years into the glaciation cycles, and have progressed far below the freeze-up level for Antarctica. We face no danger, therefore, from Antarctica melting and flooding the Earth. The Earth is too cold for that. However, we are in great danger of the Earth's cold, interglacial climate from collapsing further into glacial conditions. We are already seeing consequences of the weakening Sun, such as in the form of the weakened greenhouse effect of our atmosphere, with effects that are being measured even in Antarctica.

While all effects in climate change are blamed on manmade global warming, which isn't physically possible, the underlying cosmic cause for the climate change is being denied, such as the cause for the current climate cooling. We are in danger of our denial of this reality, because when the 'Sun' drops out of the interglacial level into glacial conditions, the step into glaciation will be big. The step will be as big as that of a person stepping off a cliff, which is never a gradual thing and has huge consequences. Ironically, no one is prepared for the consequences of the resulting glaciation climate. While we have all the resources on hand to build us a New World with technological infrastructures to evade the cosmic consequences, we find ourselves too small at heart to take the needed steps. This is where the real manmade danger lies.

- *The Author*

- Rolf A. F. Witzsche is a long-time author, researcher, and producer of more than a hundred videos. His published books comprise 14 novels, a 12 volume research series, and a large series of illustrated science books with images and transcripts of his exploration video productions. The illustrated science exploration in this book is a part of the illustrated science books series. His research and publication effort, exploring the Ice Age dynamics, as a science, began in the 1990s.

The Cover Image:

Analysis of weather station and satellite data, showing the continent-wide warming trend from 1957 through 2006.
by NASA - http://earthobservatory.nasa.gov/IOTD/view.php?id=36736

Author: Eric J. Steig (University of Washington), David P. Schneider (National Center for Atmospheric Research), Scott D. Rutherford (Roger Williams University), Michael E. Mann (Pennsylvania State University), Josefino C. Comiso (NASA Goddard Space Flight Center), and Drew T. Shindell (NASA Goddard Institute for Space Studies and Columbia University)

Table of Contents

Earth was Radically Warmer when Antarctica Froze Up

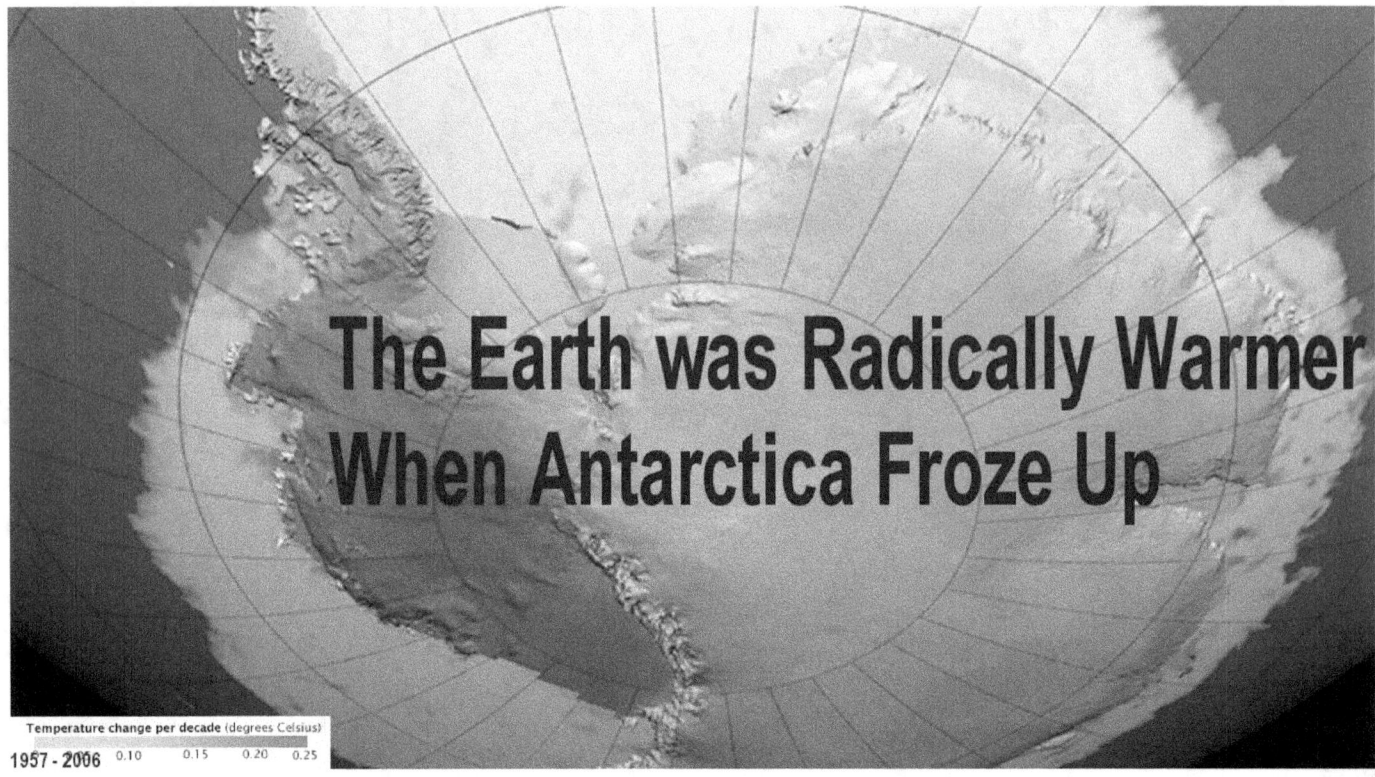

The Earth was Radically Warmer indeed, when Antarctica Froze Up so long ago. What does this mean for our time?

Antarctica froze up three quarters of the way to the bottom

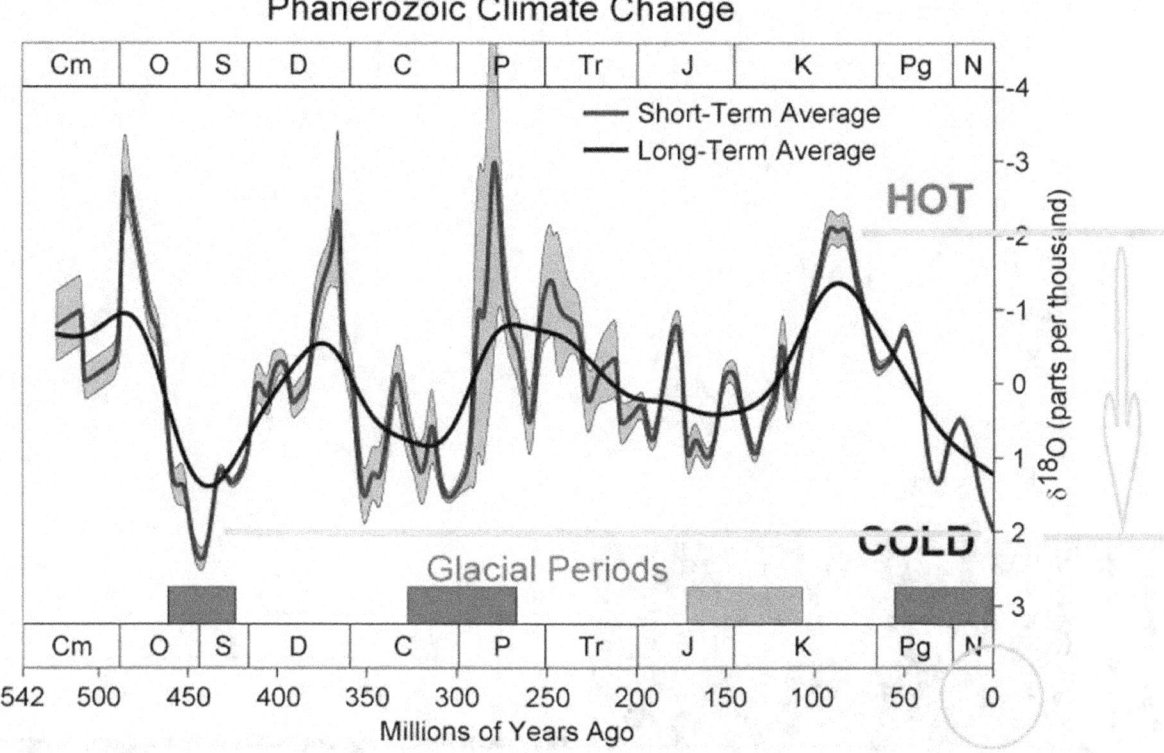

Antarctica froze up three quarters of the way to the bottom of the deep climate collapse of the last 100 million years in Phanerozoic Climate history.

Antarctica froze up when the Sun cooled sufficiently

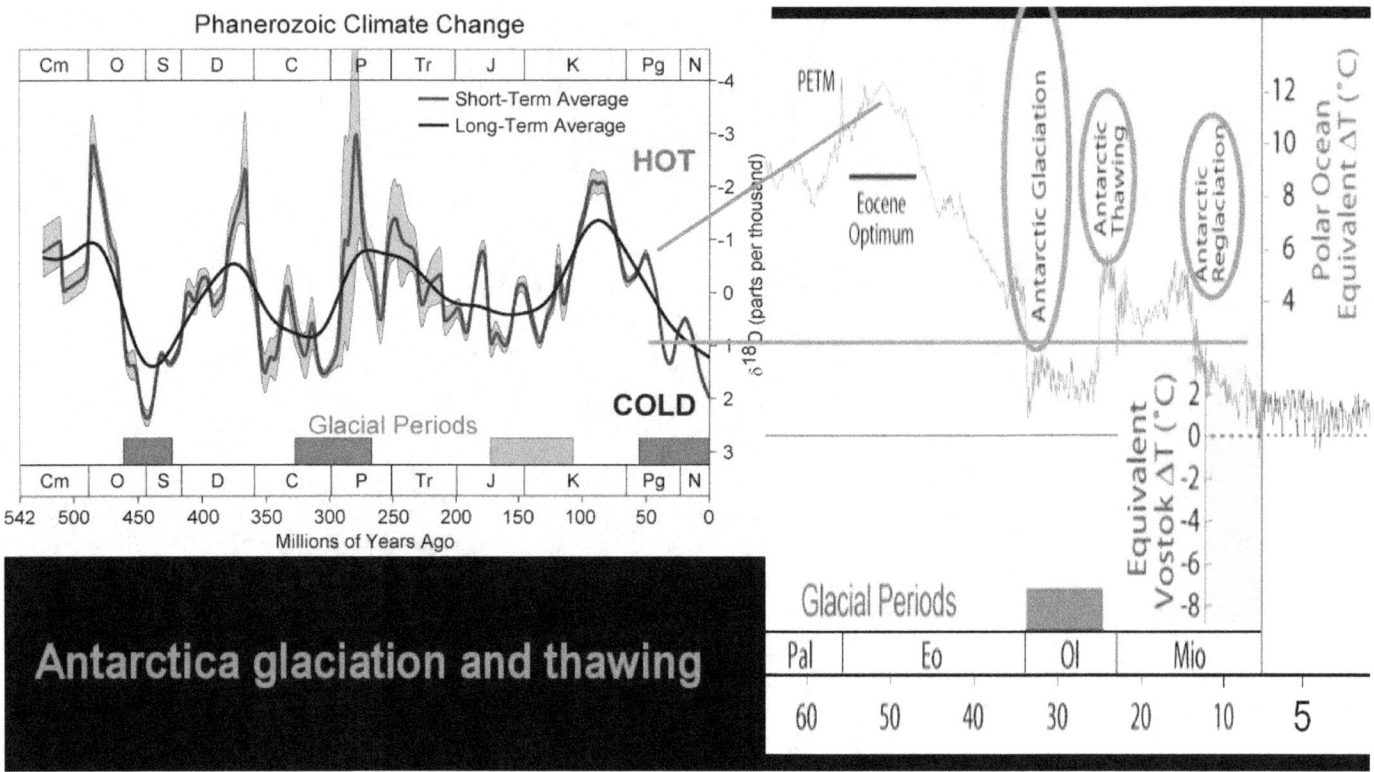

Antarctica froze up when the Sun cooled sufficiently for this to happen. This occurred roughly 32 million years ago.

Because the long-term climate collapse unfolded in steps, Antarctica had thawed out again a few million years later as the Sun became warmer for a period. After that, the Sun became colder again so that Antarctica froze up once more and remained frozen thereafter, while the Sun continued to cool.

When Antarctica froze up for a second time, roughly 12 million years ago, the climate on Earth was still radically warmer than it is in our time.

It would take another 10 million years of the Sun getting still weaker

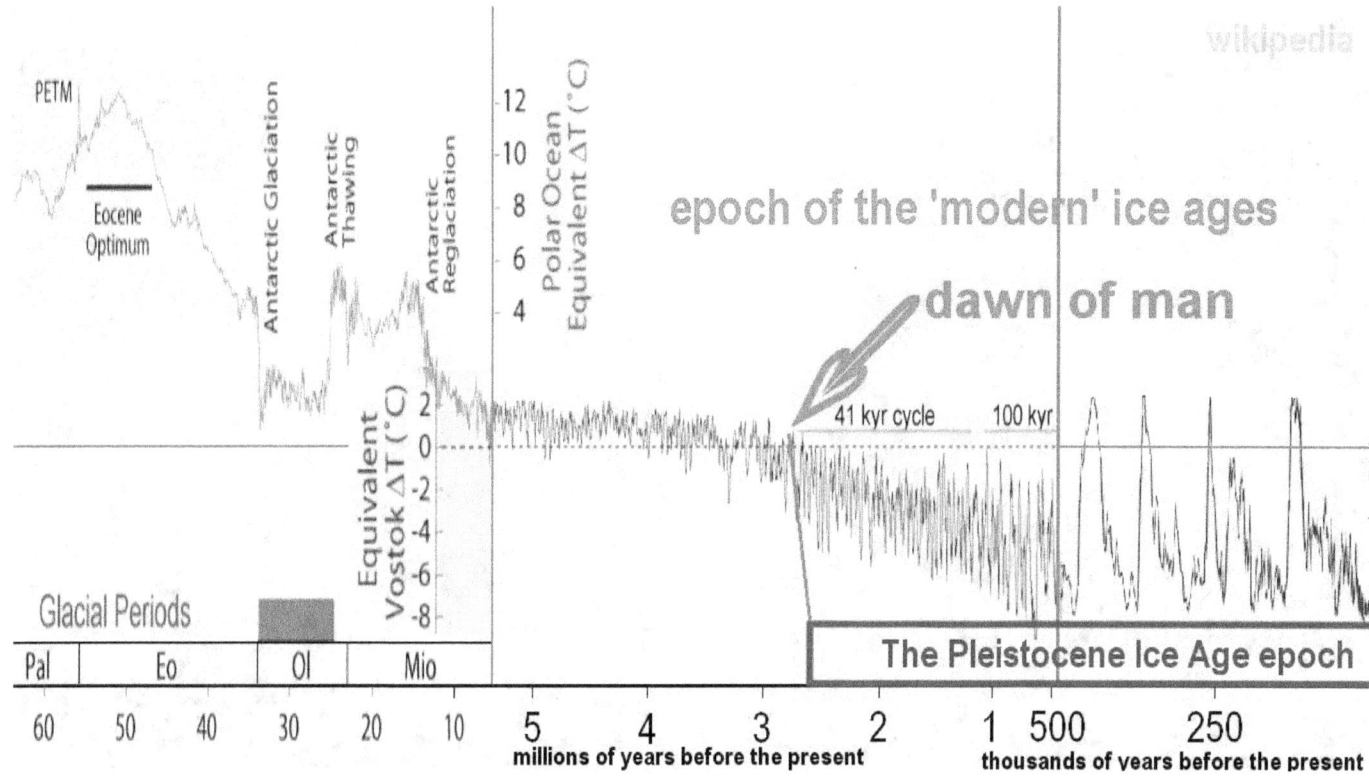

It would take another 10 million years of the Sun getting still weaker and colder, for the Ice Age glaciation cycles to begin. We are presently far below the freeze-up level for Antarctica. We face no danger, therefore, from Antarctica melting down and flooding the Earth.

While some minuscule warming of Antarctica has been measured

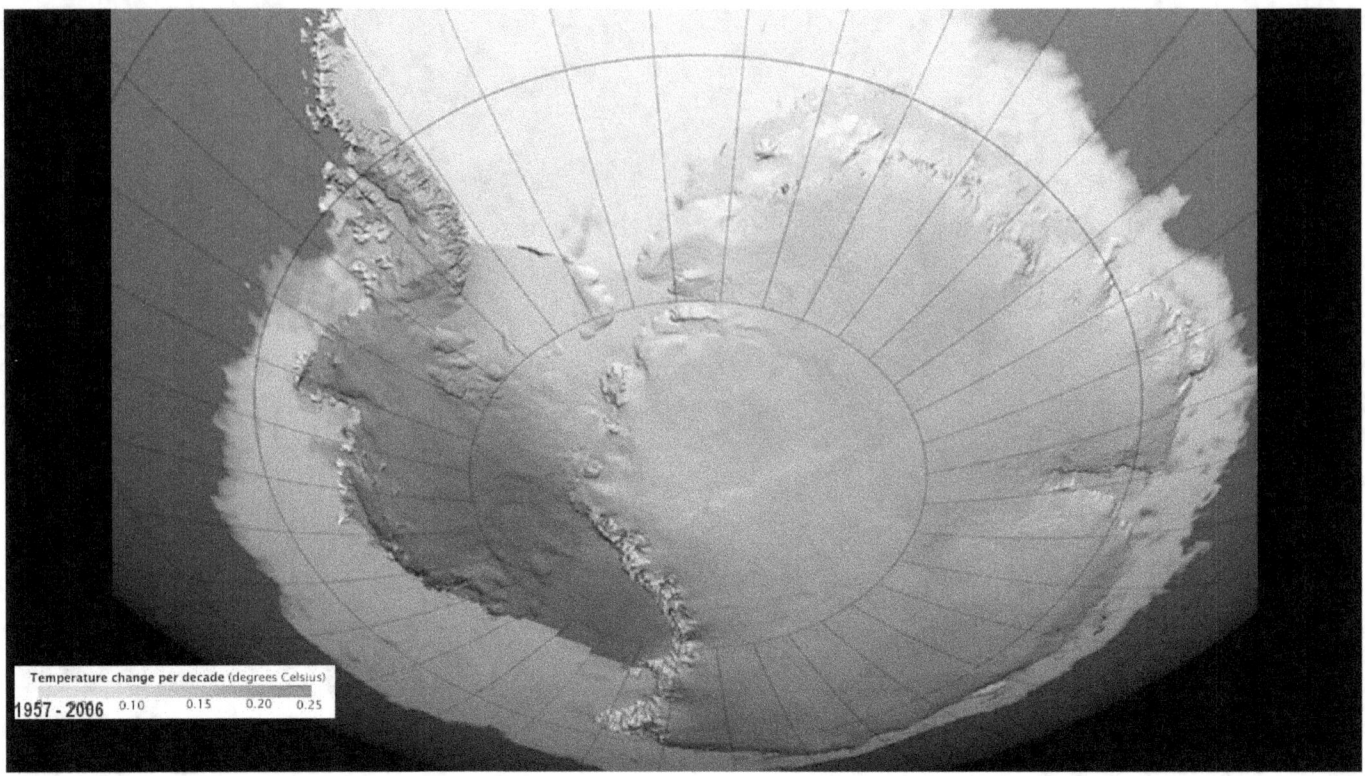

Temperature change per decade (degrees Celsius)
1957 - 2006   0.10   0.15   0.20   0.25

While some minuscule warming of Antarctica has been measured over the last 50 years, up to 2006, in the order of a few tens of a degree per decade, the measured warming should raise no concern.

The measured Arctic Warming from 1957 to 2006

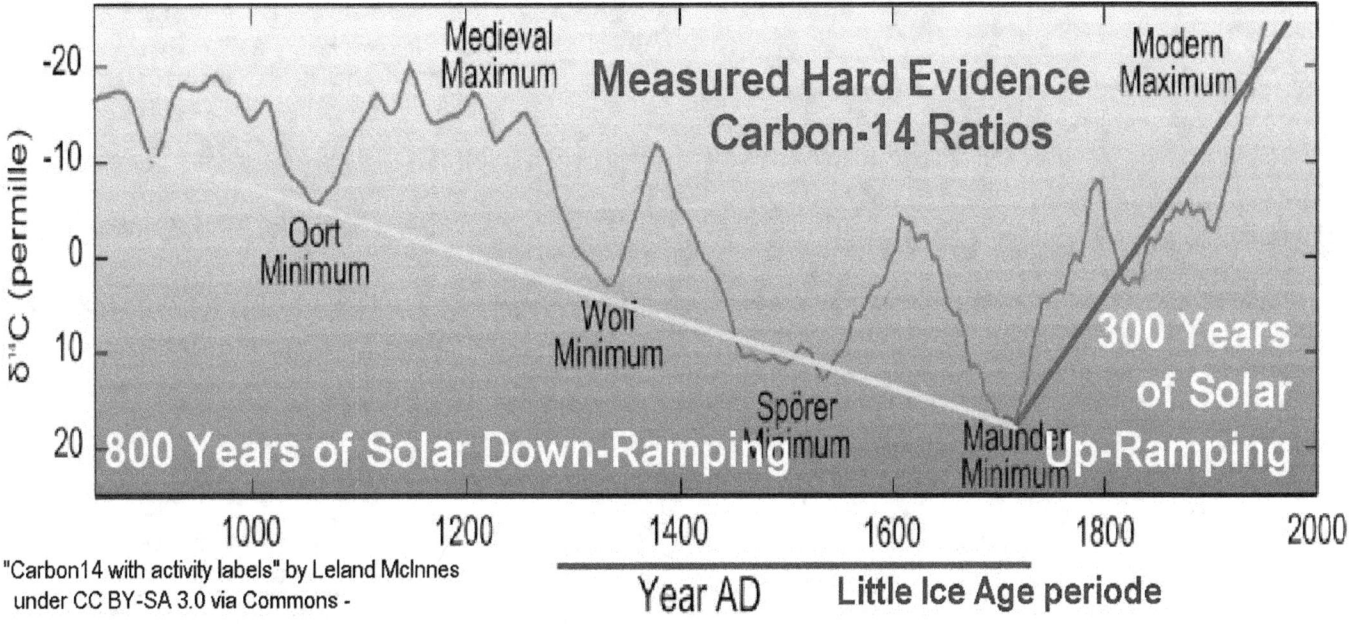

Historic Solar Activity - presented in radio Carbon-14 production ratios
This graph plots solar cosmic-ray flux, NOT earth's temperature fluctuations that follow in step.

Measured Hard Evidence Carbon-14 Ratios

Medieval Maximum

Modern Maximum

Oort Minimum

Wolf Minimum

Spörer Minimum

Maunder Minimum

800 Years of Solar Down-Ramping

300 Years of Solar Up-Ramping

δ¹³C (permille)

"Carbon14 with activity labels" by Leland McInnes under CC BY-SA 3.0 via Commons -

Year AD   Little Ice Age periode

This is so, because the measured Arctic Warming from 1957 to 2006 falls well within the timeframe of the great global warming by the Sun that we have measured evidence of in terms of increased solar activity, which broke us out of the Little Ice Age in the early 1700s

Since the solar global warming from the Little Ice Age on has run its course

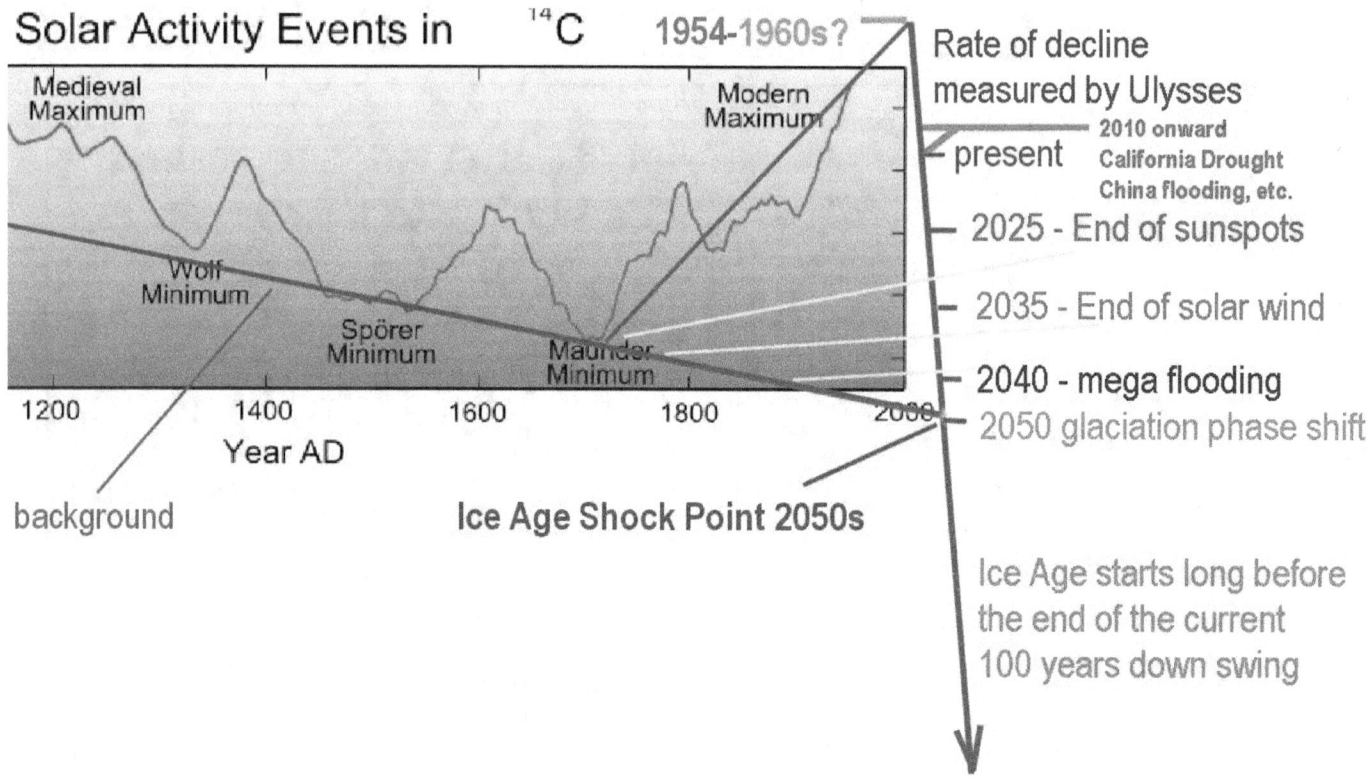

Since the solar global warming from the Little Ice Age on has run its course, and is now reversing like a falling stone, we face no danger in the future of the Earth overheating and of Antarctica melting. This is true, because the collapse in solar activity is reflected in the typically corresponding climate collapse on Earth. This is what is now ongoing, which we have measurements of.

A secondary feature, which mimics global warming

NASA   Credits: University of Durham/Pippa Whitehouse

The presently ongoing climate collapse also has a secondary feature, which mimics global warming, and is often cited as proof for global warming. While the landscape of Antarctica continues to be buried in ice and snow, measurements indicate that continuous ice losses are occurring. This is measured by measuring the out-flow of Ice from the continent.

Measured in units of millimetres of sea-level contribution, per decade

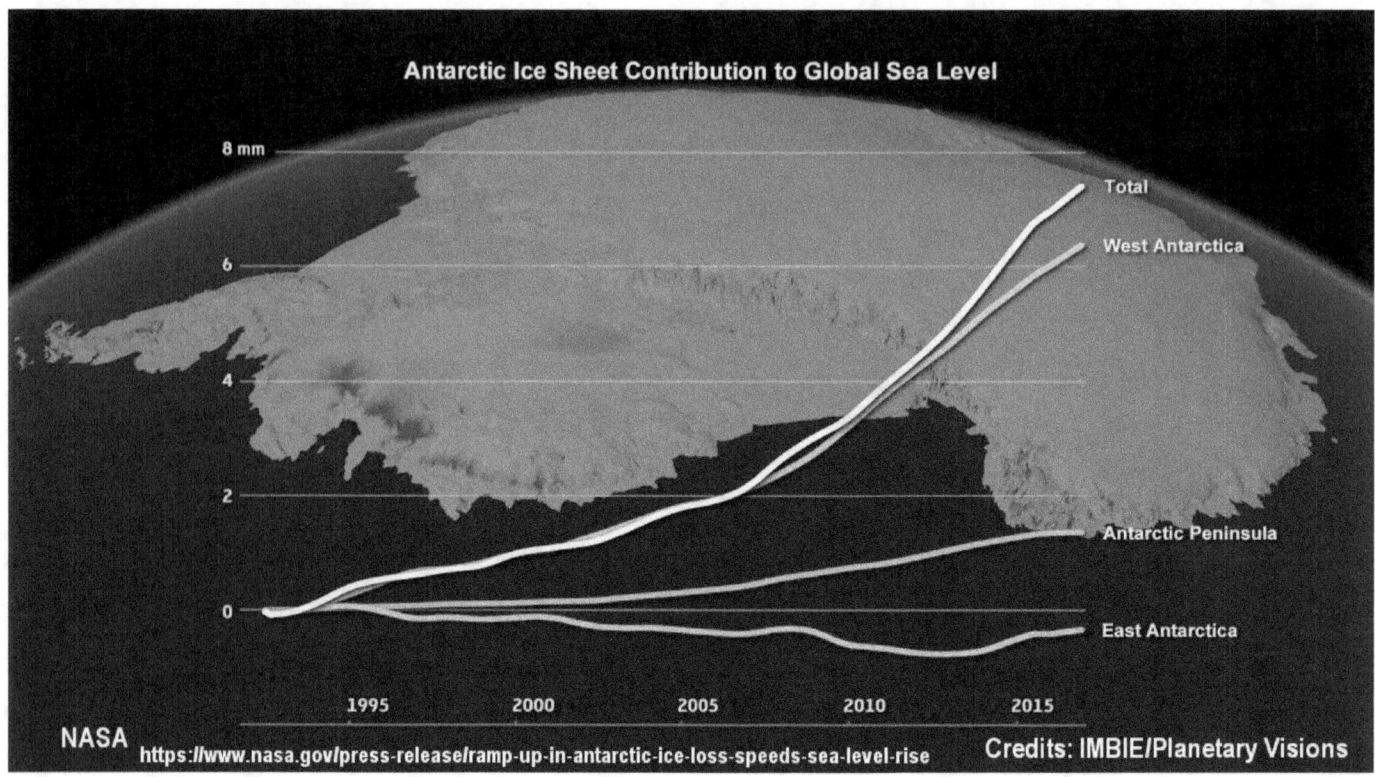

While the outflow of rivers is often measured in units of cubic meters per second, the Antarctic outflow is measured on a different scale. It is measured in units of millimetres of sea-level contribution, per decade. The measured result adds up to 7 millimetres of sea-level contribution over the span of 20 years.

Please note that the outflow from Antarctica has slightly increased from 2007 onward.

The result of the weakening greenhouse effect of the atmosphere

The moderating greenhouse effect of the atmosphere narrows the cosmic temperature extremes to a nicely liveable climate.

Greenhouse effect produced by water vapor in the atmosphere

without the greenhouse effect of the Earth's atmosphere:
**night temperature -170 decrees C
day temperature +117 degrees**

Earth's greenhouse effect is diminished by cosmic-ray increase

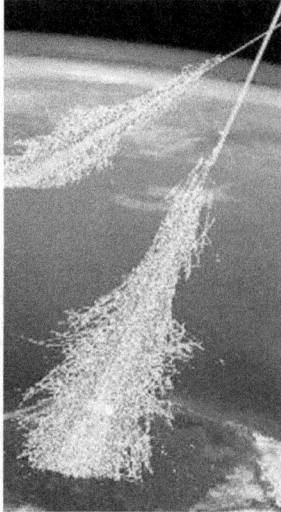

cloud nucleation reduces water vapor: deeper droughts and lesser greenhouse

other greenhouse contributions
CO_2 greenhouse contribution

cosmic-rays increase cloud nucleation

This increase of the outflow is evidently the result of the weakening greenhouse effect of the atmosphere by larger volumes of solar cosmic-ray flux that increase cloudiness, which lowers the water-vapor density in the air that furnishes 90% of the greenhouse effect. The reduced greenhouse effect enables larger temperature extremes to occur.

In Antarctica, the land of the midnight Sun

In Antarctica, the land of the midnight Sun, the reduced greenhouse effect would give the polar regions a stronger solar exposure during the summer months when the Sun never sets. The reduced greenhouse effect became more prevalent from 2007 onward when solar activity was sharply reduced, according to the sunspot numbers. This is what we see reflected in the measured ice flow out of Antarctica.

A high-precision picture of changes in ice-sheet motion

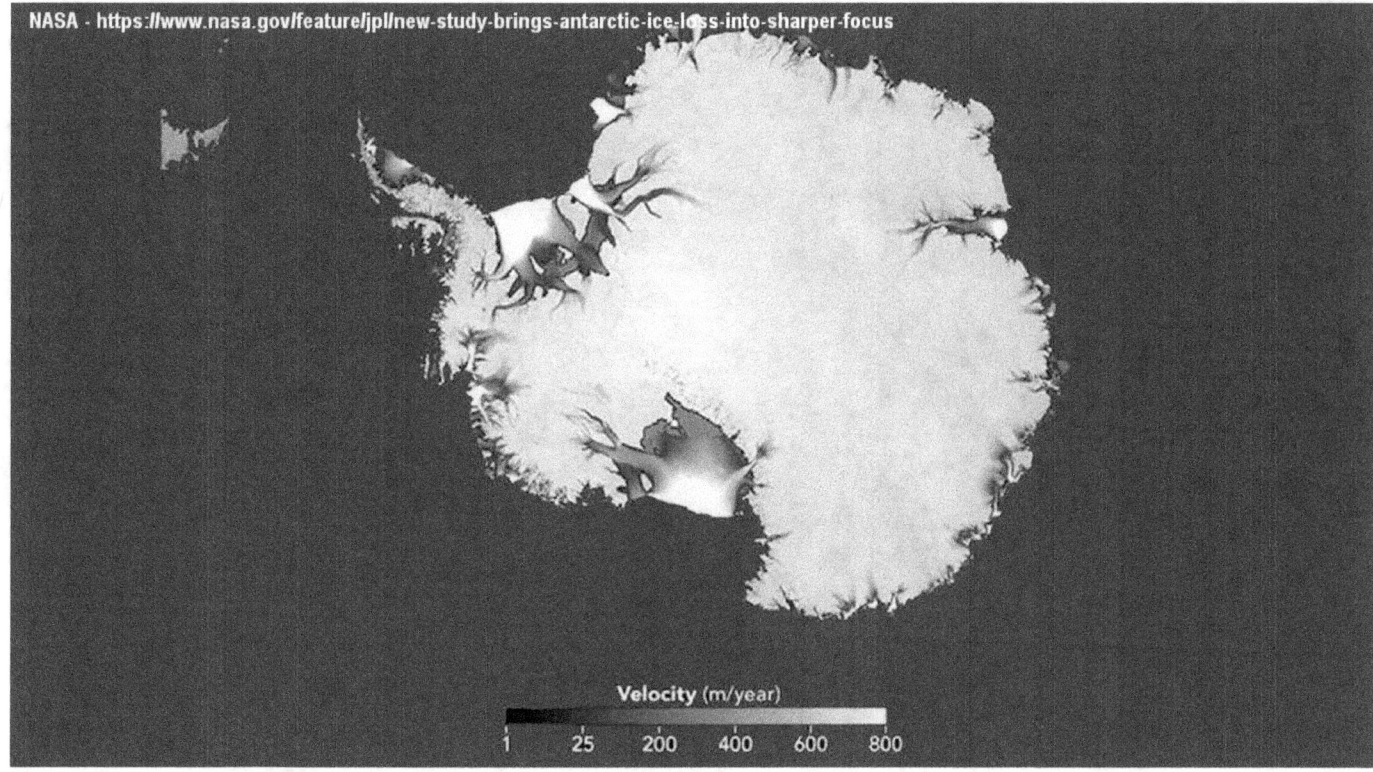

A new study by NASA has crunched ten years of data from hundreds of thousands of images from NASA's Geological Survey satellite, and has produced a high-precision picture of changes in ice-sheet motion.

This miniscule 1.8% increase over the span of 10 years

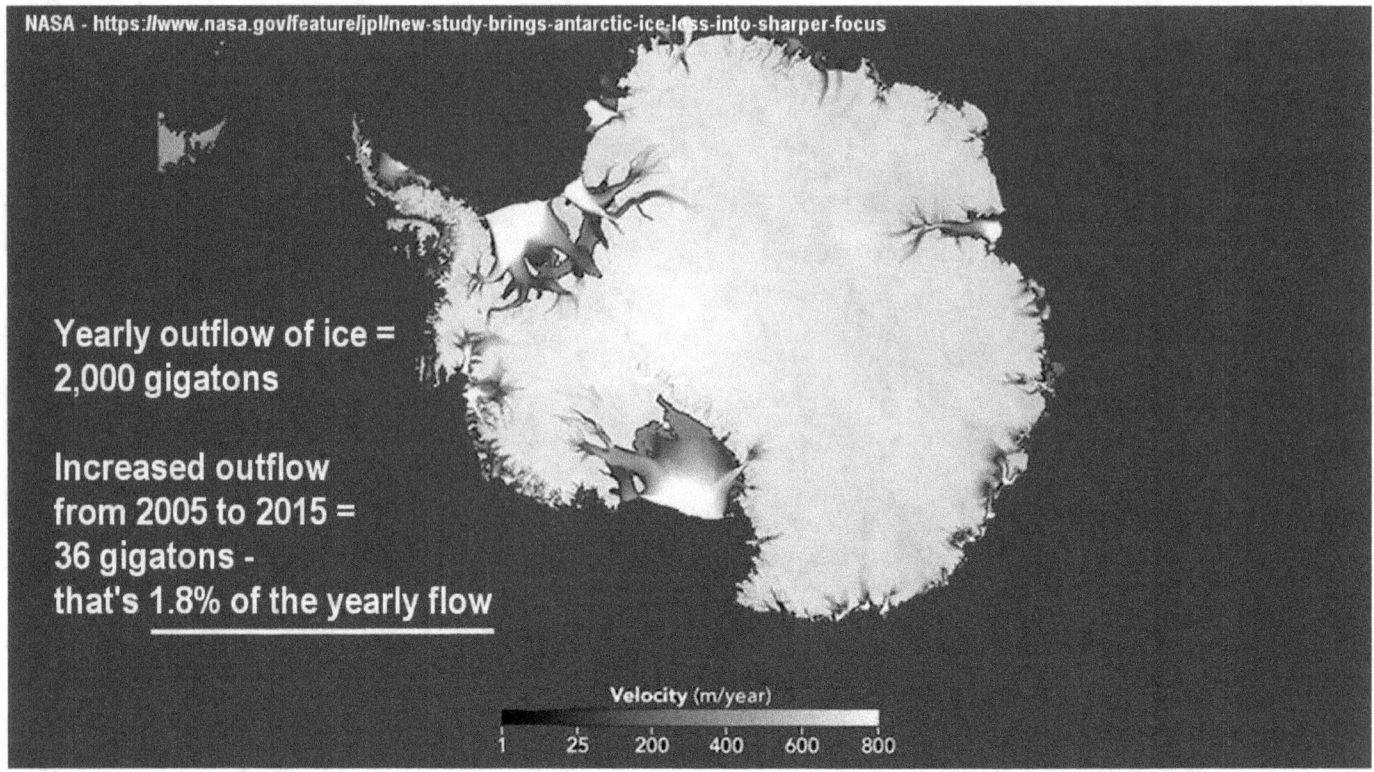

The computed data reveal that typically 2,000 gigatons of ice, flow out of Antarctica every year.

The computed data also revealed that the outflow has increased over the years. An increase of 36 gigatons has been computed for the 10-year period till 2015 . This miniscule 1.8% increase over the span of 10 years falls well within the range of change that one would expect to result from the reduced greenhouse effect that occurred in this period.

But what of it? Society has no cause to be concerned about this, for reasons of the minuscule scale of the computed ice loss.

The public has been carefully taught to be alarmed

NASA - Earth image on September 21, 2005 with the full Antarctic region visible

The public has been carefully taught to be alarmed over the increasing outflow of ice from Antarctica, which it has been instructed to see in terms of rising sea levels, resulting from manmade global warming.

This hyped-up sense of alarm is artificial. In real terms global warming isn't happening, because it is impossible. Global cooling is happening instead, and increased precipitation is happening.

If the increased precipitation would be factored into the studies, the studies might reveal that no actual net-loss of ice flowing out from Antarctica has occurred.

This doesn't mean that there is no climate change happing

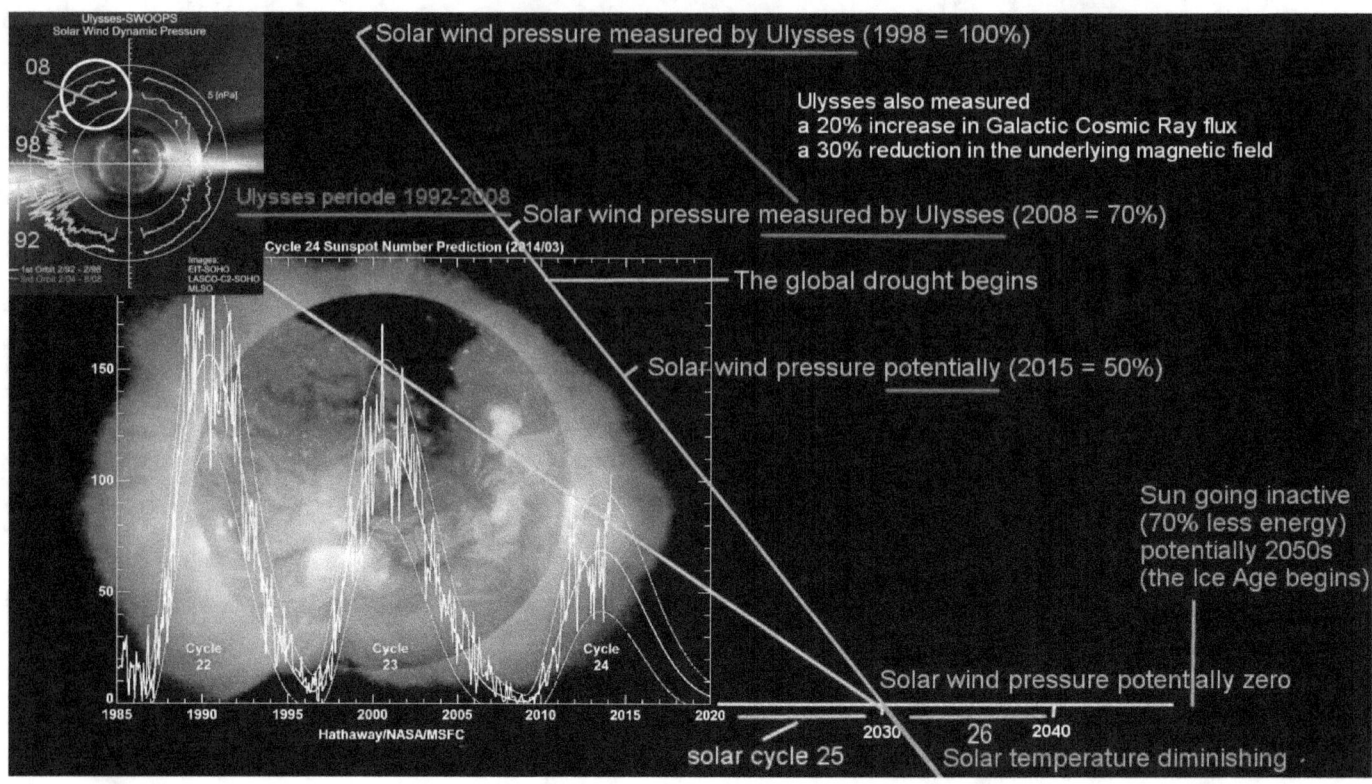

This doesn't mean that there is no climate change happing on the Earth. Huge climate change is happening. But this isn't talked about. It is effectively hidden, though it real and it is more scary than all the artificial scare scenarios combined. And the biggest scary aspect in all this is, that society has the power as human beings to evade the cosmic consequences that loom before it, but finds itself too small in its ignorance, to act. It is thereby set on a path of committing collective suicide.

The cause for the weakening greenhouse effect

The moderating greenhouse effect of the atmosphere narrows the cosmic temperature extremes to a nicely liveable climate.

Greenhouse effect produced by water vapor in the atmosphere

without the greenhouse effect of the Earth's atmosphere:
night temperature -170 decrees C
day temperature +117 degrees

Earth's greenhouse effect is diminished by cosmic-ray increase

cloud nucleation reduces water vapor: deeper droughts and lesser greenhouse

other greenhouse contributions
CO2 greenhouse contribution

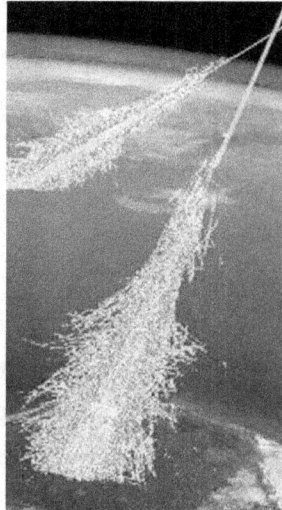

cosmic-rays increase cloud nucleation

For example, it is known, or should be known, that the cause for the weakening greenhouse effect, which is reflected in the increased rate of ice out-flow from Antarctica, is the direct result of the fast collapsing solar activity level that enables larger volumes of solar cosmic-ray flux to affect the Earth. Shouldn't the reduced greenhouse effect raise some concern?

The fast collapsing solar activity should cause urgent concern

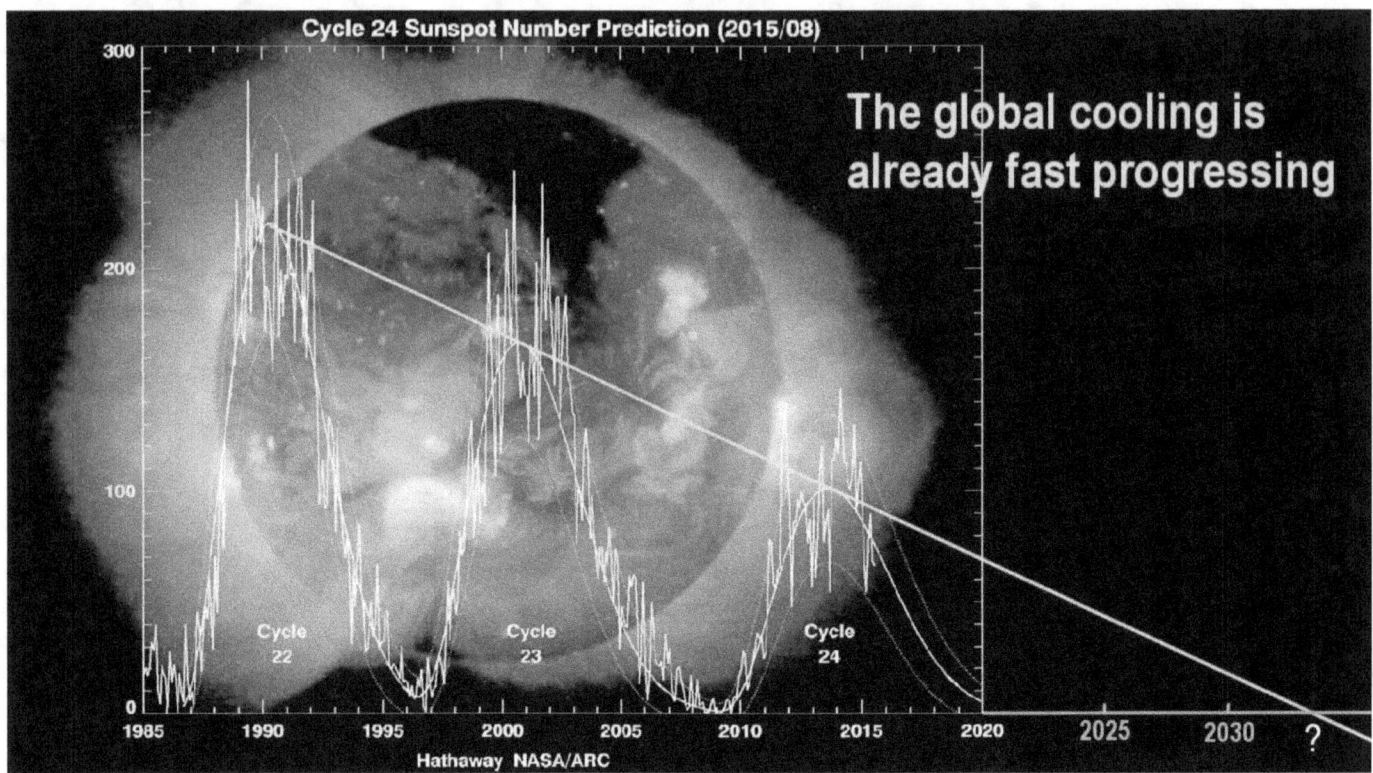

The fast collapsing solar activity, which is known and well documented, should cause urgent concern all across the world, because the collapsing solar activity tells us that the interglacial climate is rapidly ending.

We are already in the boundary zone to the next Ice Age

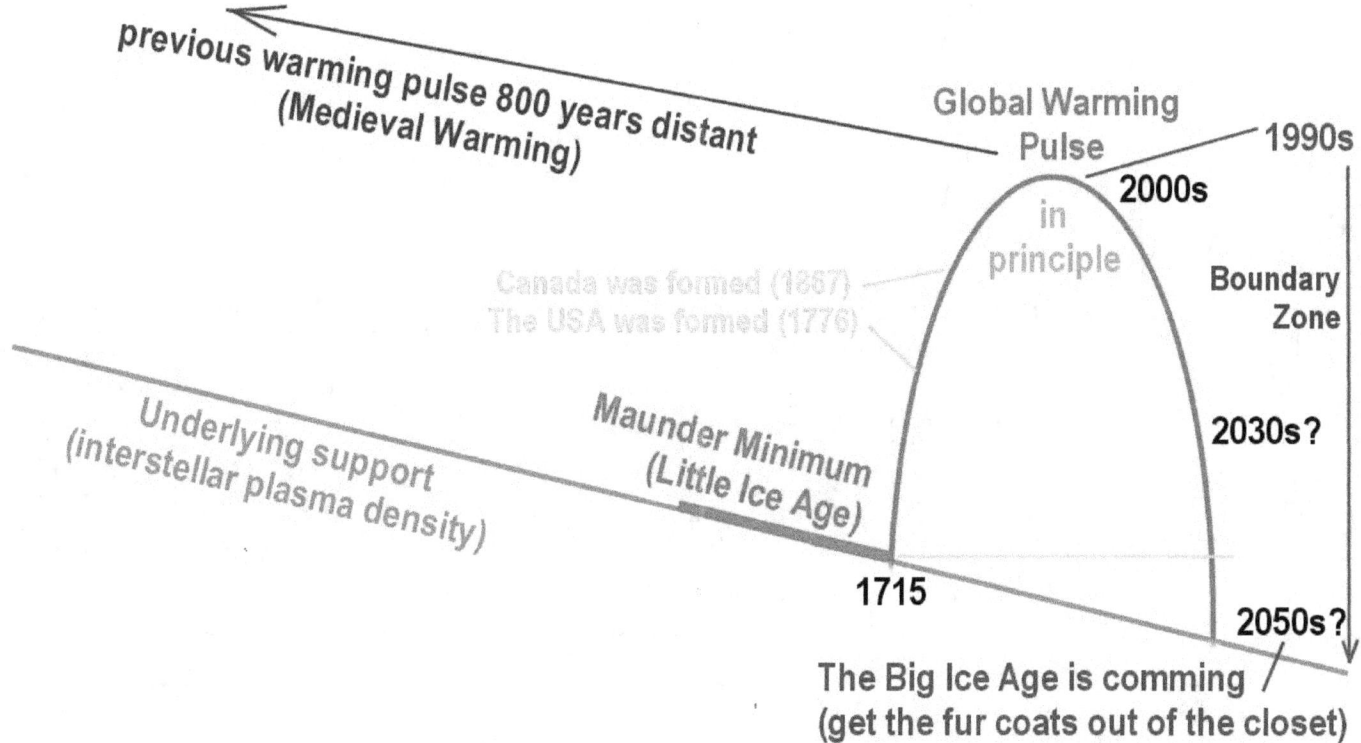

It tells us that we are already in the boundary zone to the next Ice Age, which may be upon us in the 2050s. We have numerous measurements made to support this recognition. The recognition presents an existential challenge to the whole of humanity. Ironically, society responds by closing its mind to this challenge that threatens its very existence.

While the ice-loss from Antarctica poses absolutely no danger

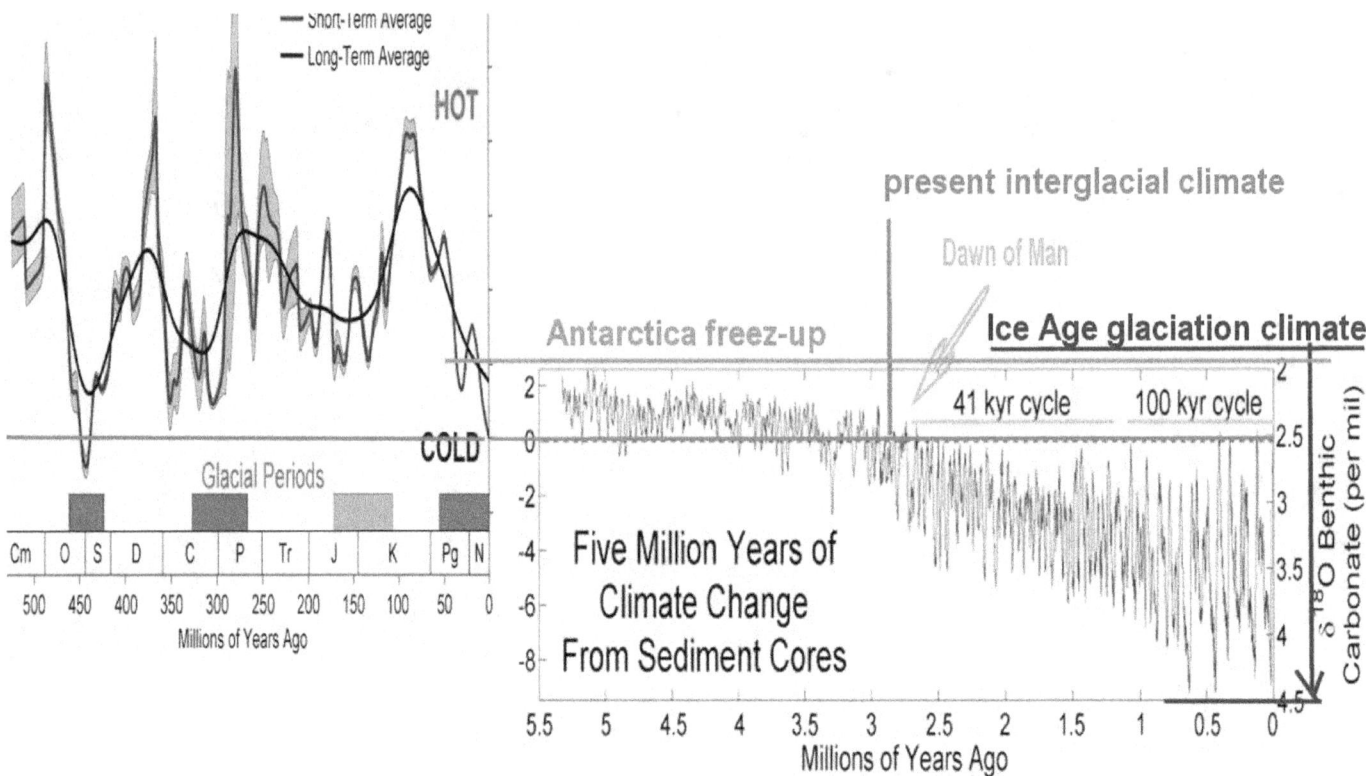

While the ice-loss from Antarctica poses absolutely no danger to our world, we face immensely great dangers in the context of the cold climate that we are in. Note, the light blue line across the image marks the current interglacial climate. Its level is far lower, which means colder, than the level when Antarctica froze up.

Now look at what lies below the blue line. That's where the Ice Age glaciation unfolds. In comparison with what is known about the glaciation climate, our current blue-line interglacial climate is like a summer breeze.

The deep cold glaciation climate becomes our future when the phase shift happens that 'drops' us below the interglacial, into the next Ice Age glaciation phase.

All the climate variations that have been experienced

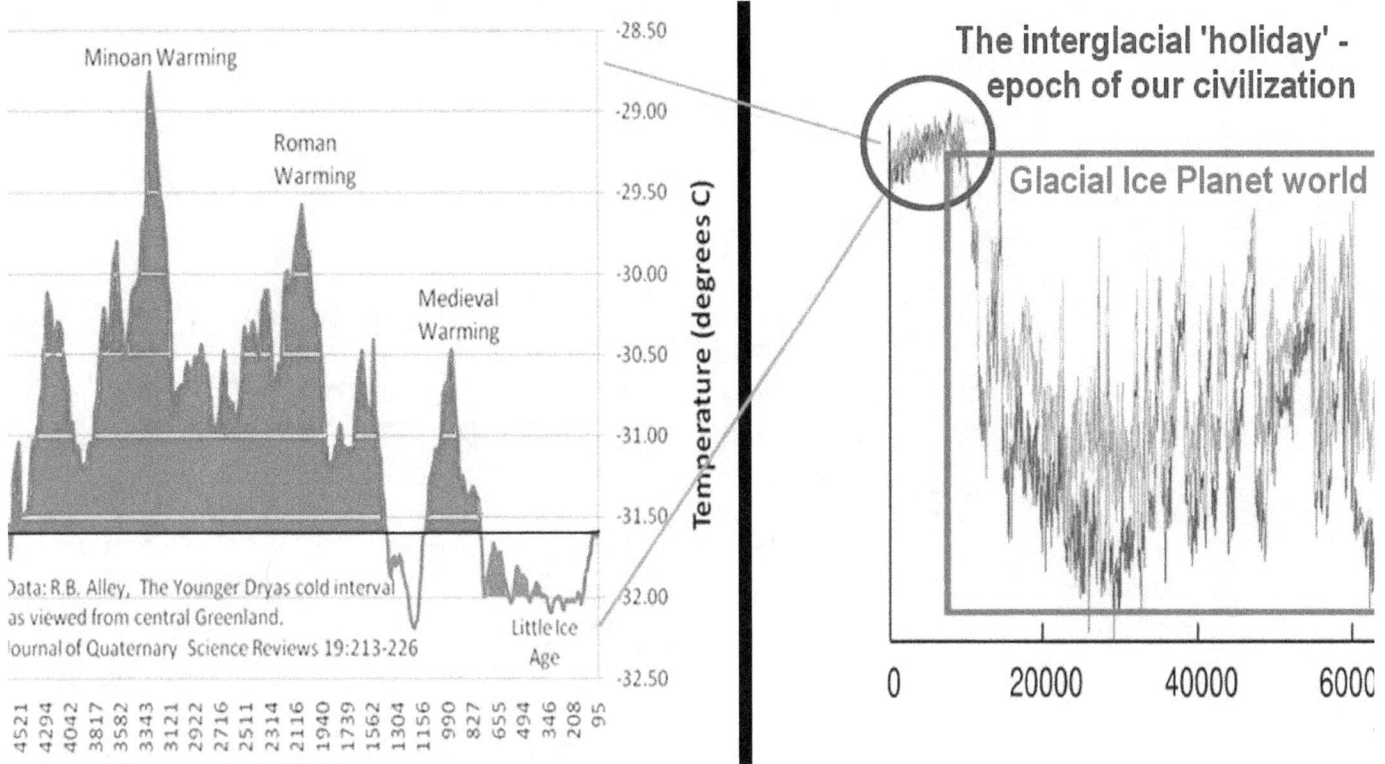

Data: R.B. Alley, The Younger Dryas cold interval as viewed from central Greenland. Journal of Quaternary Science Reviews 19:213-226

The blue circle at top center is at the blue line. In the circle the current interglacial climate unfolds, and has so for the entire span of the development of civilization. All the climate variations that have been experienced, that we have records of, from the big warming events to the Little Ice Age events, are all compressed within that blue circle.

Extreme danger begins when the Sun takes a further step down

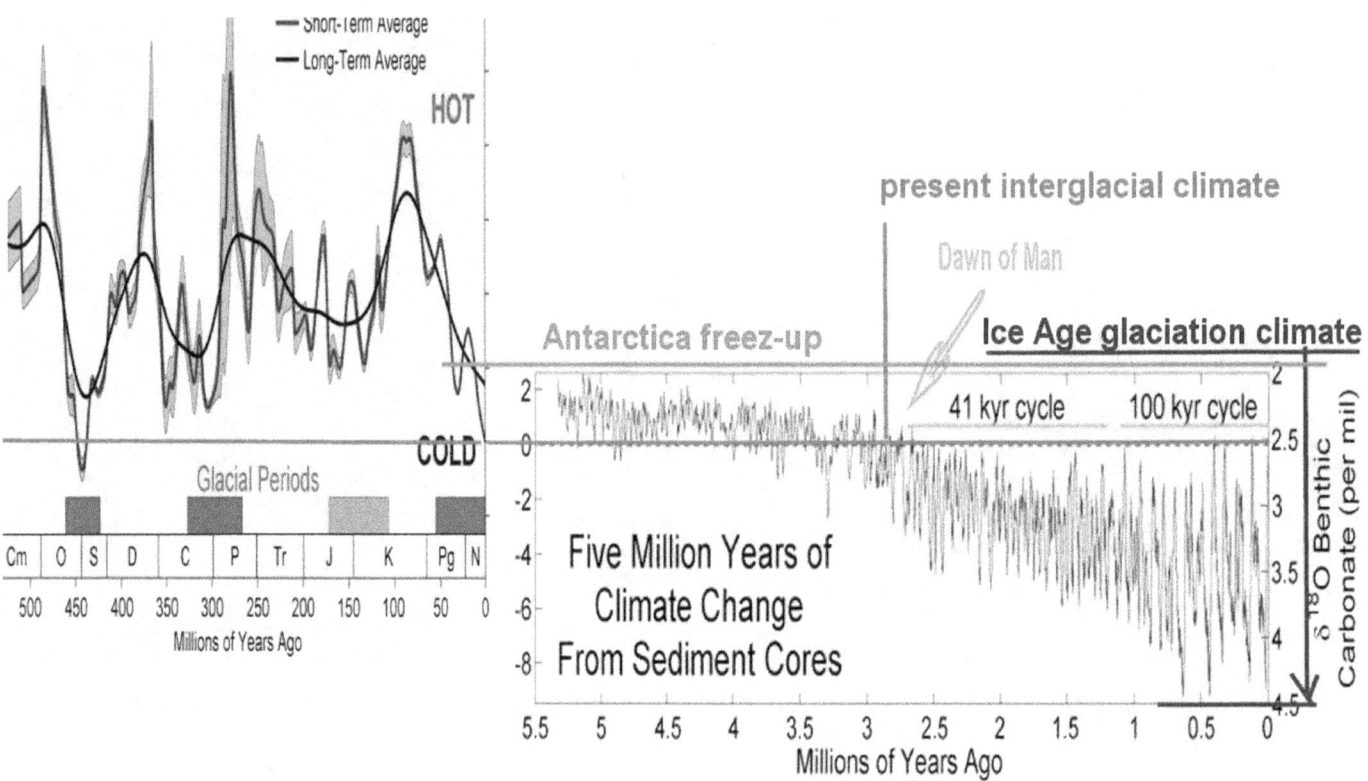

Extreme danger begins when the Sun takes a further step down on the path of its cooling, below the blue line, to where the next glacial period unfolds, potentially in the 2050s. Stepping below the blue line, by the weakening Sun, won't be a small step, because small steps are no longer possible below the blue line.

When the solar system weakens to the point that the Primer Fields collapse

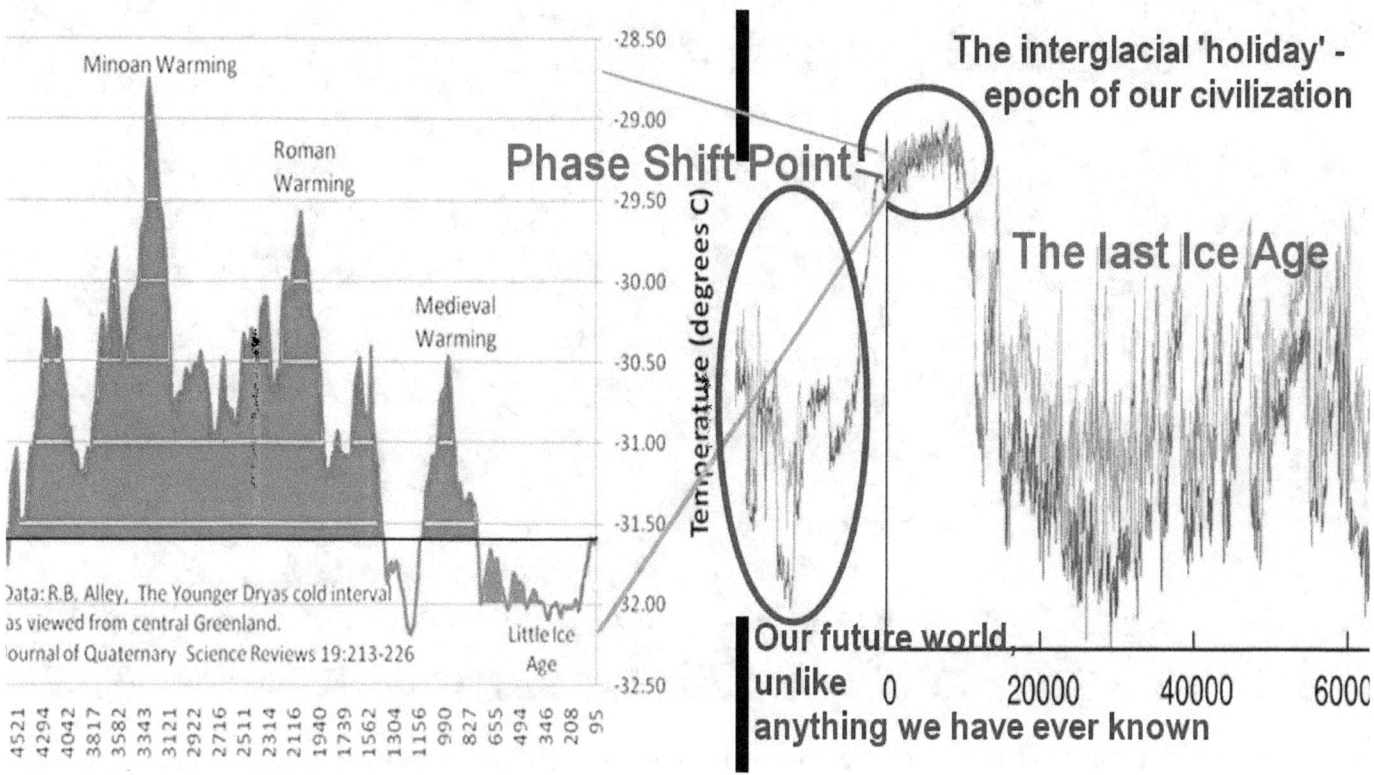

As we cross below the blue line, or below the blue circle, which happens when the solar system weakens to the point that the Primer Fields collapse that keep the Sun in its presently high-powered mode, then we enter a radically different world that is as different as night and day. When we drop out of the blue circle, we drop deep, in giant leaps, like leaping of a high cliff that is never a gradual process.

An in-between state is NOT possible

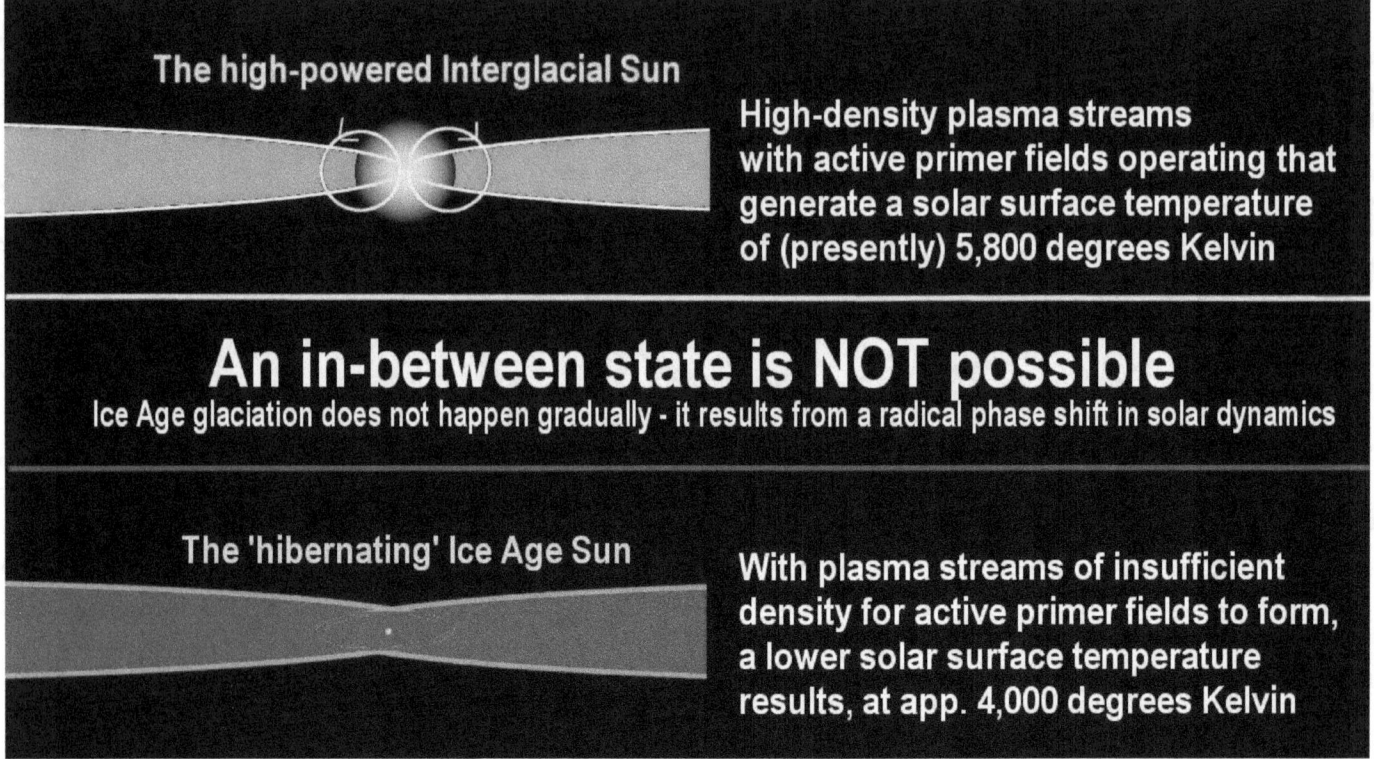

An in-between state is NOT possible when one is leaping off a cliff. Likewise, Ice Age glaciation does not happen gradually. It results from a radical phase shift in solar dynamics.

When the phase shift happen by which the primer fields vanish, the Sun drops into low-power hibernation mode, and we on the Earth begin to face unprecedented cold climates almost immediately. The Earth becomes then an entirely different world in an extremely rapid transition.

During glaciation conditions, the winter sea ice extent

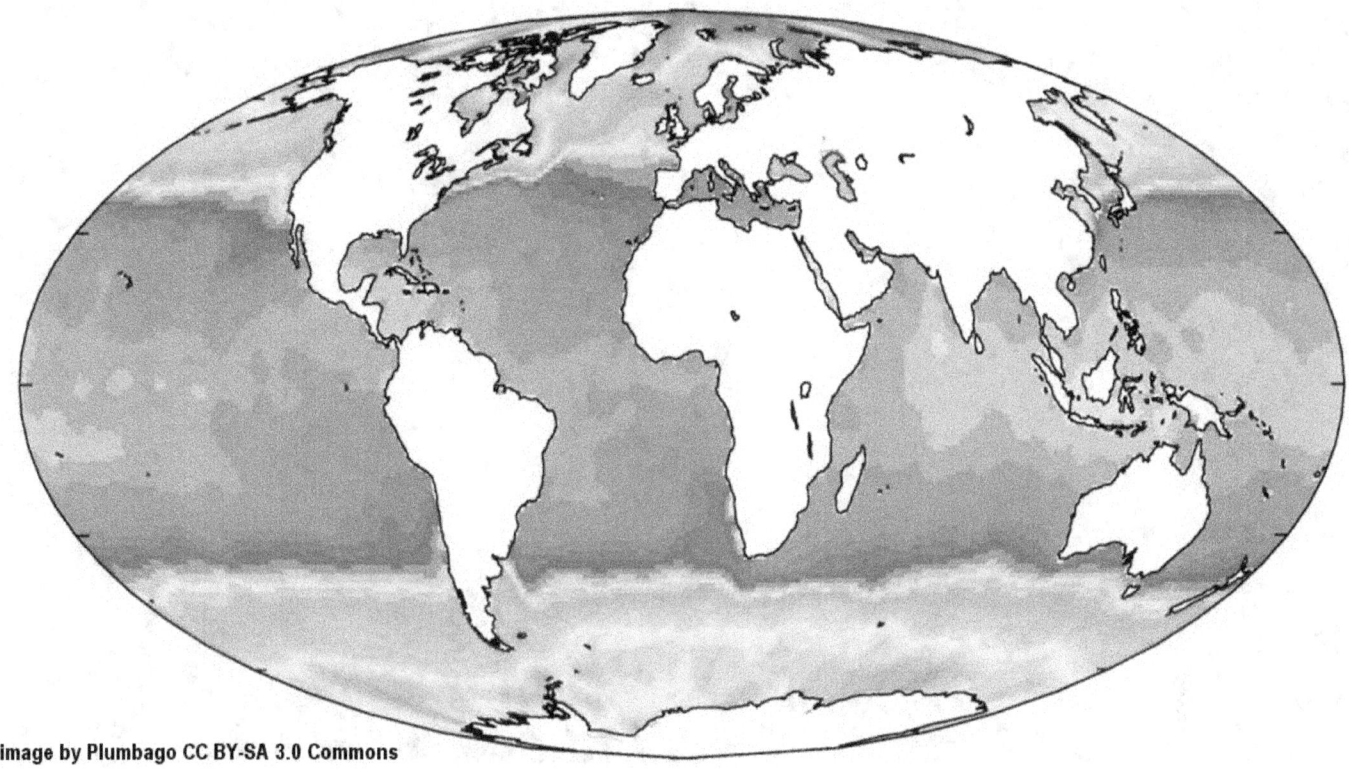

image by Plumbago CC BY-SA 3.0 Commons

During glaciation conditions, the winter sea ice extent, represented by the blue line, will then reach as far north as South Africa, South America, Australia, and New Zealand.

In the North, the winter sea ice extent will likely reach as far south as Mexico, Morocco, and engulf almost all of China.

The cold areas will not be limited to the Big Ice Sheets

The cold areas will not be limited to the Big Ice Sheets, but will extend all the way to the red circle, the permafrost circle. The Arctic circumference becomes thereby extended all the way to the sub-tropics. In this unfolding process, Canada, Europe, Russia, and possibly also China and the USA will cease to exist as their territories become claimed by the cold, and agriculture becomes disabled.

It is known that during the last glacial period, the area around Beijing was permafrost country, a poor place for agriculture.

When Antarctica froze up, 12 million years ago

NASA - Earth image on September 21, 2005
with the full Antarctic region visible

When Antarctica froze up, 12 million years ago, the climate was likely much too warm for the continent to be encircled with the vast fields of sea ice that we see today, and with the giant ice shelves that are formed by the out-flow of glaciers floating on the surface of the sea.

However, those big phenomena that we see happening today will likely appear tiny in comparison with what we will see under full glaciation conditions.

While the forming of sea ice does not affect the sea levels, because sea ice is formed out of the water of the sea, the sea-ice extent provides nevertheless a measure for the intensity of glaciation and its impact on human living. Under glaciation conditions the sea ice will likely cover the entire area that is visible in this image, and possibly extend beyond it.

The sea ice extent will likely reach as far as South Africa

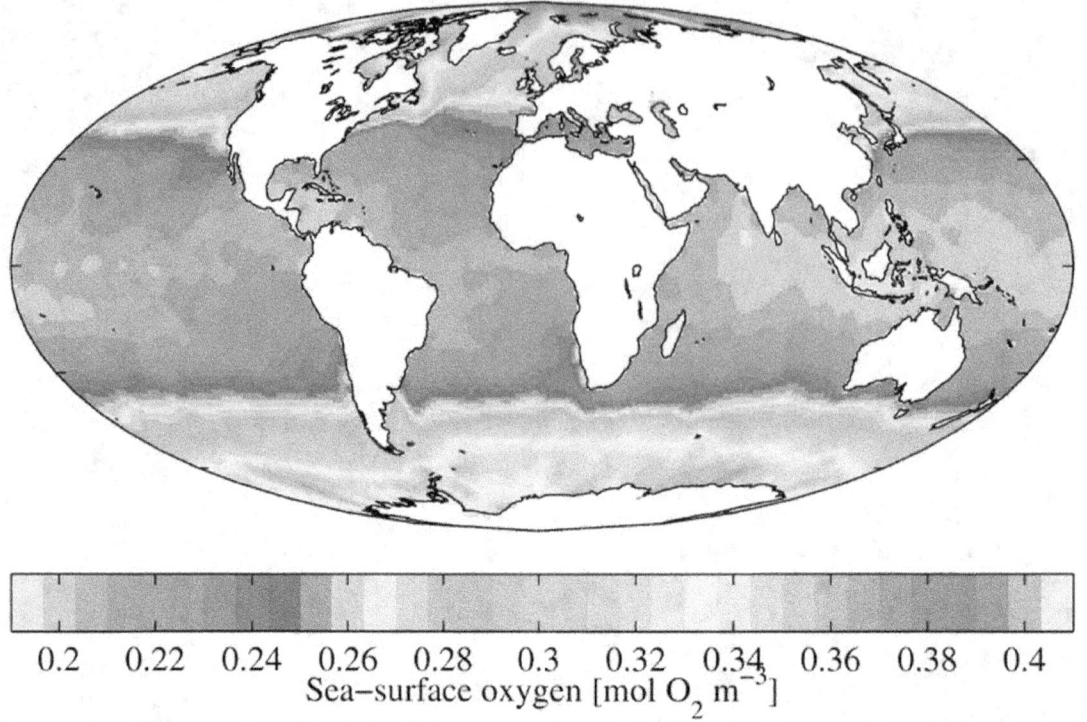

Sea–surface oxygen [mol O_2 m^{-3}]

Dissolved oxygen levels at the ocean's surface: (data: World Ocean Atlas 2009; photo credit: Plumbago; Wikipedia Commons) CC BY-sa 3.0

As I said before, the sea ice extent, represented by the blue line, will likely reach as far as South Africa, and from the North to Morocco. The delineation shown here is measured in sea surface oxygen concentration, which is climate sensitive. The blue line happens to match the theorized winter sea-ice extent during the previous glaciation cycle.

The deep ice sheets only form on land, or in shallow waters

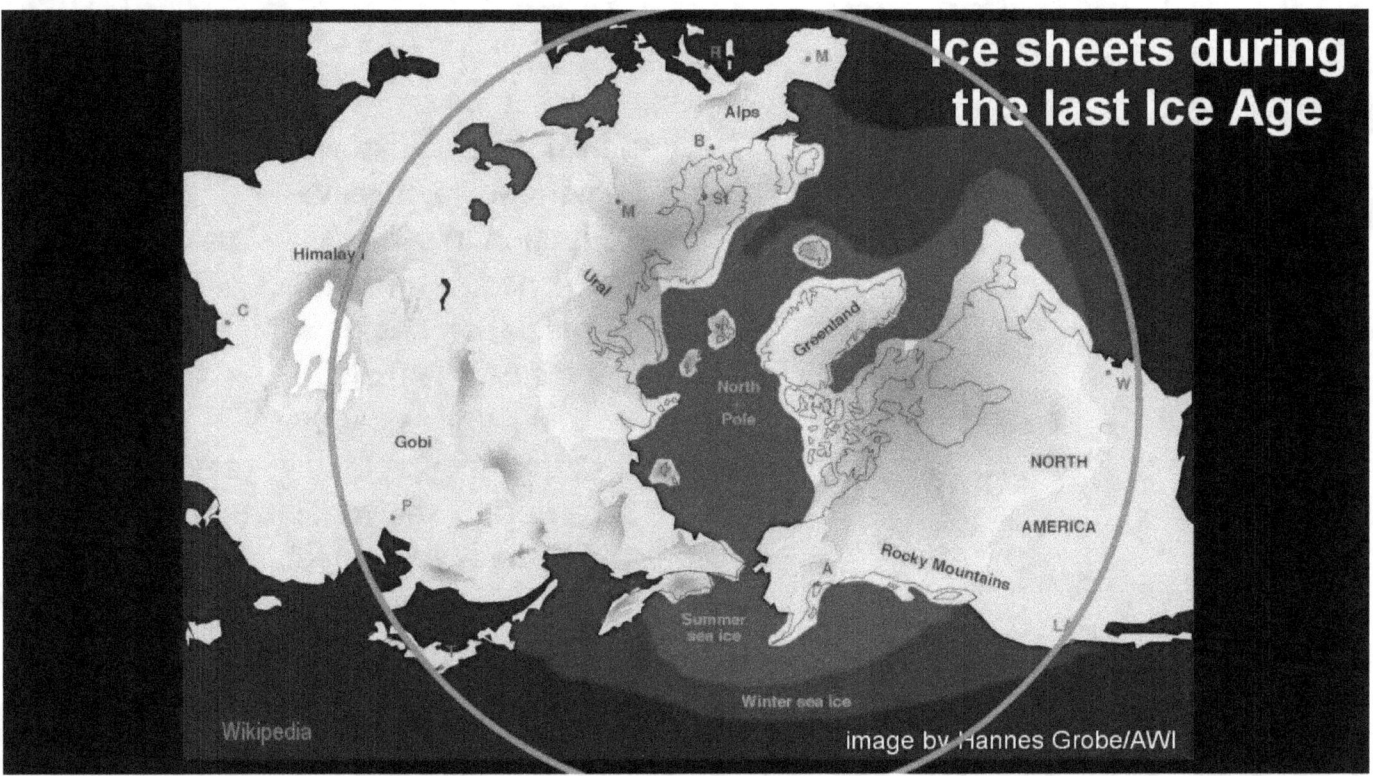

The deep ice sheets, in contrast, only form on land, or in shallow waters. On land, the thickness of the ice is limited by its weight. Under extreme pressures ice becomes viscose and begins to flow. The limit appears to be in the range of 3,500 meters. Large parts of Europe and North America would have been buried under deep ice. We will likely see the beginning of the ice build-up before the Ice Age actually starts, when the climate becomes cold enough that the winter snow no longer melts.

During the last Ice Age the sea level was reduced by 130 meters

Expect a near-term sea-level reduction

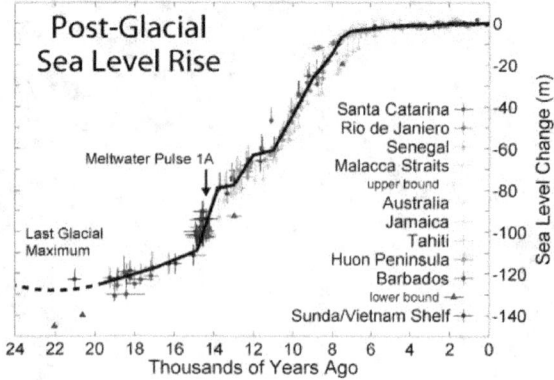

The danger is that we will experience a massive reduction in sea level in the near term as the re-glaciation begins with the Ice Age Transition now in progress.
Picture a loss of only 20 meters
A powerfull new renaissance will be needed to meet the physical challenge for infrastructures

Wikipedia

With the transfer of water onto the land, the sea levels begin to change, and not in small measures. The changes won't be measured in millimetres over decades. They will be measured in meters. During the last Ice Age the sea level was reduced by 130 meters, or 425 feet.

Under Ice Age conditions precipitation is reduced by 80%,

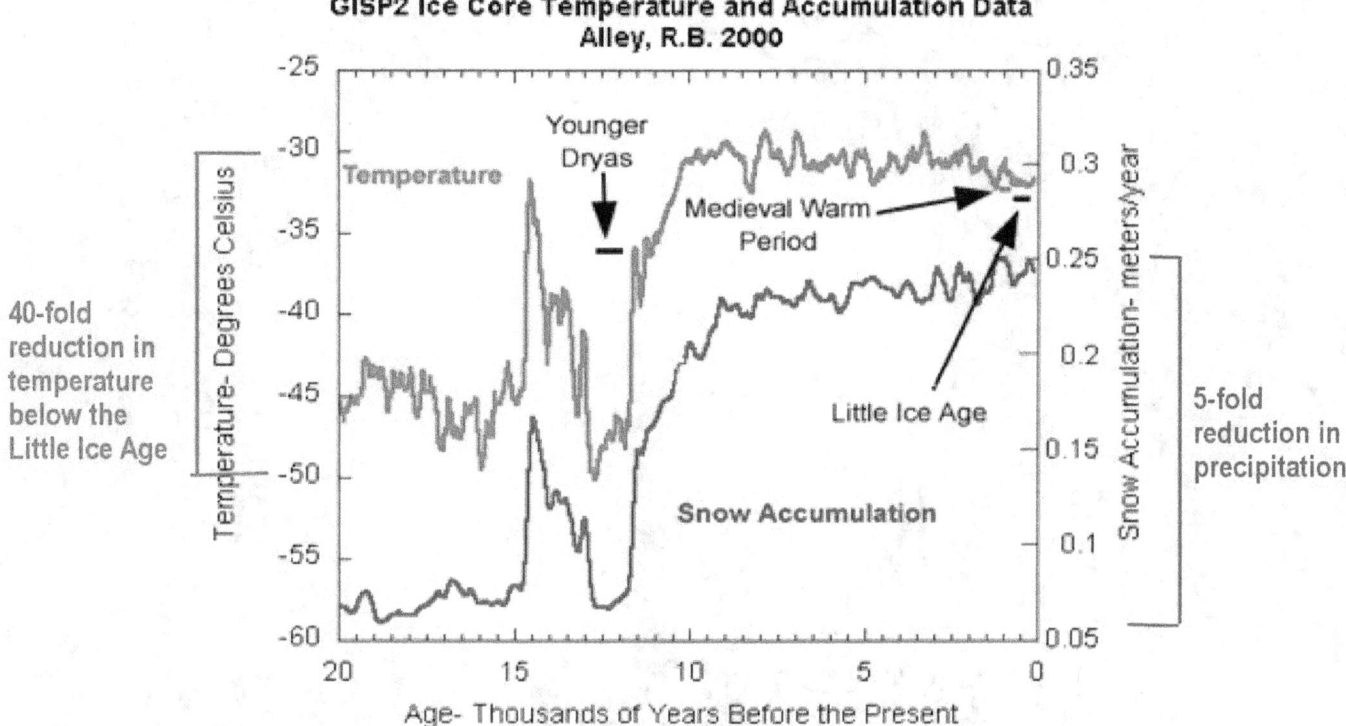

It probably took thousands of years of 'snowfall' to lay up so much water on land in the form of ice under Ice Age conditions when precipitation is reduced by 80%, as had been the case according to glacial measurements.

Ice fog, instead of as rain or snow

During glacial conditions, precipitation is likely carried into the polar regions in the form of ice fog, instead of as rain or snow. The ice fog would likely have obscured the features of the Earth similar to a veil, far more than today's cloudiness does when seen from space. This may need to be considered for future designs of agriculture.

With the plasma solar system now fast diminishing

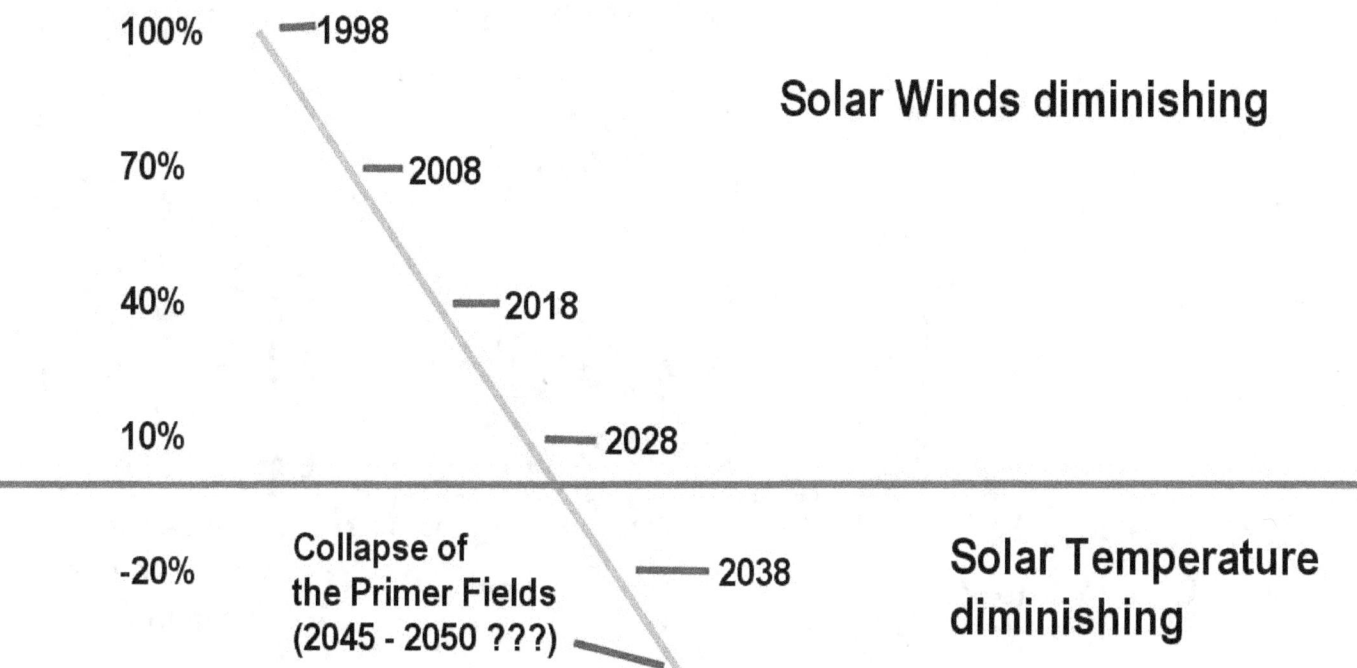

Solar Winds diminishing

100%	1998
70%	2008
40%	2018
10%	2028
-20%	Collapse of the Primer Fields (2045 - 2050 ???) 2038

Solar Temperature diminishing

That's the environment that we are getting into, potentially in the 2050s, with the plasma solar system now fast diminishing. The solar wind is diminishing. Solar activity is diminishing. Even the solar cycles are diminishing. The Earth is getting colder. Agricultures are affected. Solar cosmic rays are increasing. Cloudiness is increasing. The greenhouse is diminishing.

The reduced greenhouse effect that we are beginning to experience

The moderating greenhouse effect of the atmosphere narrows the cosmic temperature extremes to a nicely liveable climate.

Greenhouse effect
produced by
water vapor
in the atmosphere

without the greenhouse effect of the Earth's atmosphere:
night temperature -170 decrees C
day temperature +117 degrees

Earth's greenhouse effect is diminished by cosmic-ray increase

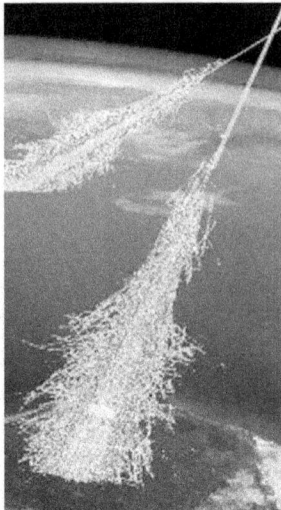

cloud nucleation reduces water vapor: deeper droughts and lesser greenhouse

cosmic-rays increase cloud nucleation

other greenhouse contributions

CO2 greenhouse contribution

The reduced greenhouse effect that we are beginning to experience, all over the world, not just in Antarctica, as a result of the increased cosmic-ray flux, is just another fringe effect of the many types of fringe effects that we experience while the boundary zone unfolds to the next Ice Age.

An example is the big winter blizzard in April

Spring Blizzard Xanto, Snow in Africa, Arctic Ice Recovers, Media Distracts (581)

Jordan Hall via LSM
Chadron, Nebraska
April 13, 2018

BLOWING SNOW

ICY ROADS

Blizzard conditions shut down

roads in Nebraska

The Weather Channel

An example is the big winter blizzard in April that swept across the North American grain belt at a time when spring planting should be in progress.

Another example is that the Sun lost its north-pole magnetic field

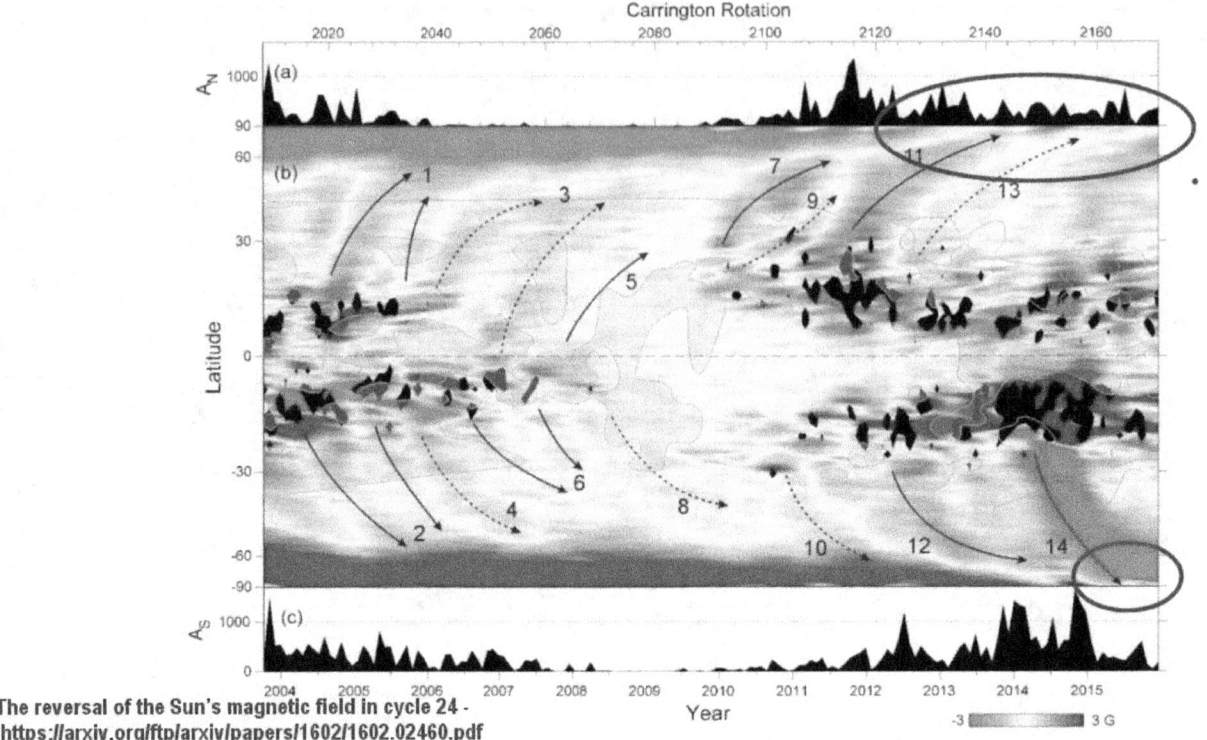

The reversal of the Sun's magnetic field in cycle 24 -
https://arxiv.org/ftp/arxiv/papers/1602/1602.02460.pdf

Another example is that the Sun lost its north-pole magnetic field. It simply vanished in 2014 when it should have reversed polarity.

The phase shift into glaciation isn't scary by itself

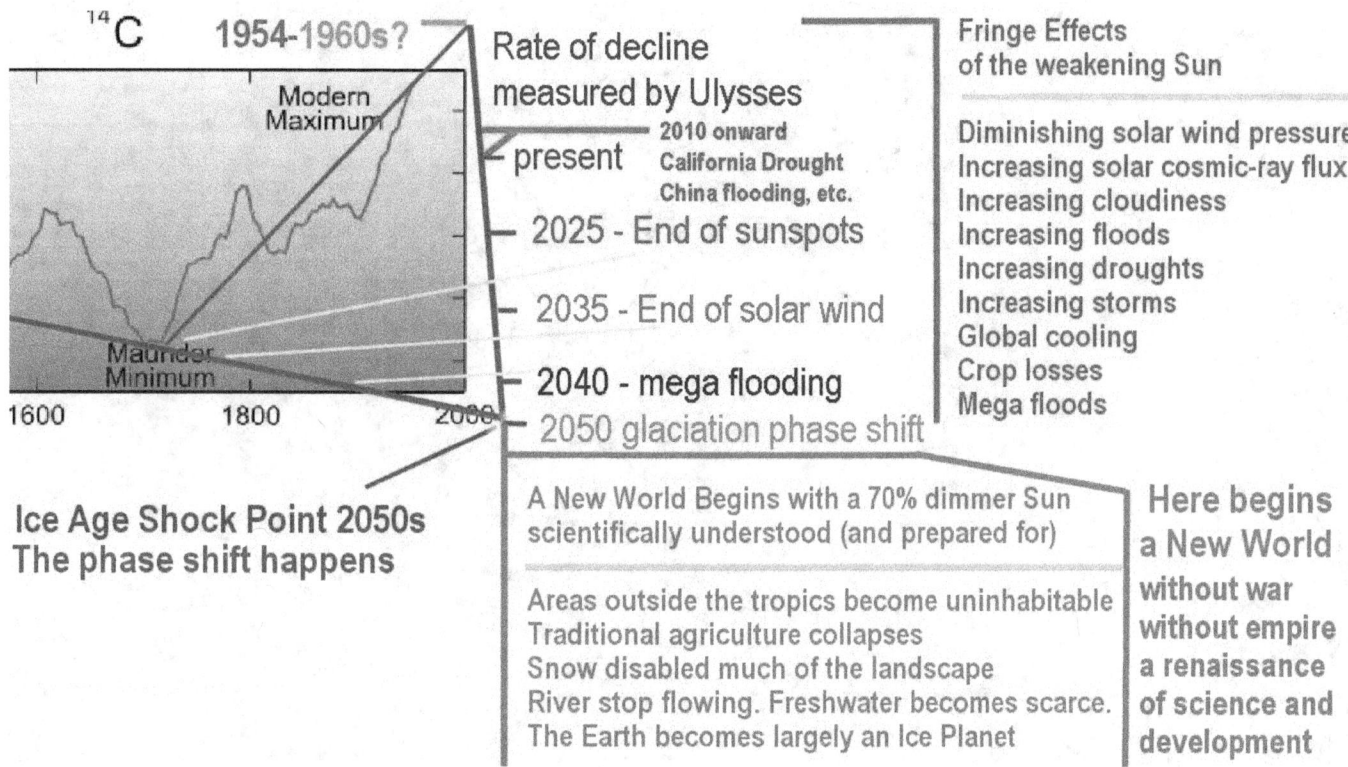

Ice Age Shock Point 2050s
The phase shift happens

Rate of decline measured by Ulysses

- present — 2010 onward — California Drought, China flooding, etc.
- 2025 - End of sunspots
- 2035 - End of solar wind
- 2040 - mega flooding
- 2050 glaciation phase shift

Fringe Effects of the weakening Sun

Diminishing solar wind pressure
Increasing solar cosmic-ray flux
Increasing cloudiness
Increasing floods
Increasing droughts
Increasing storms
Global cooling
Crop losses
Mega floods

A New World Begins with a 70% dimmer Sun scientifically understood (and prepared for)

Areas outside the tropics become uninhabitable
Traditional agriculture collapses
Snow disabled much of the landscape
River stop flowing. Freshwater becomes scarce.
The Earth becomes largely an Ice Planet

Here begins a New World without war without empire a renaissance of science and development

Tragically, the many increasing fringe effects don't seem to rouse anyone's attention. No preparations are being considered at the present time, for what the 'writing on the wall' is projecting for our future. No Plan-B is being considered, much less implemented. Nothing is being done.

The phase shift into glaciation isn't scary by itself,

we can prepare us for the consequences with technological infrastructures.

Our refusal to respond to the cosmic dynamics

- our refusal to assure our continued living -

that's what is scary - really scary - a denial of our humanity!

If society wants to worry about something big

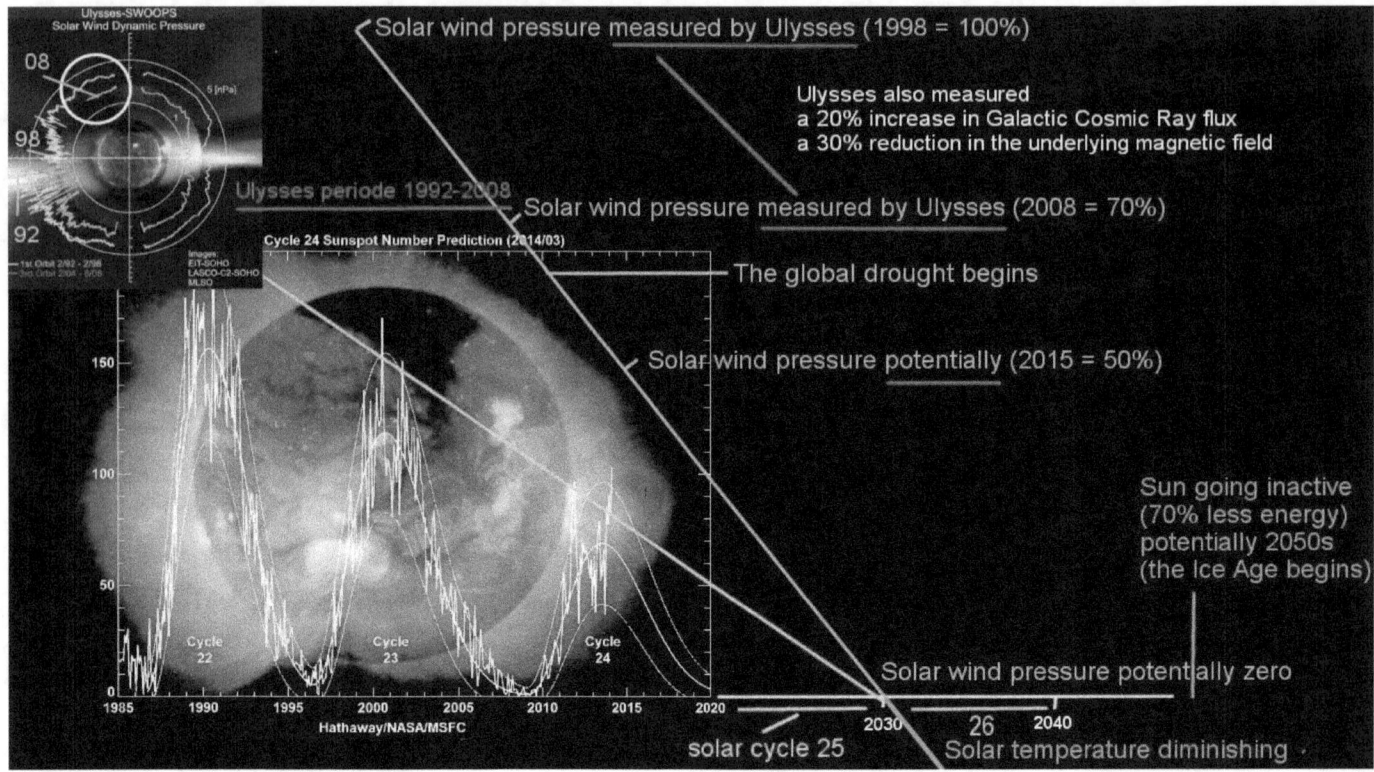

We see the writing on the wall in terms of massive scientific data, but we ignore the measurements when they don't match political objectives or private opinions. Today's cultivated ignorance, is where the greatest danger to humanity is presently located.

If society wants to worry about something big that is actually real, then it should worry about its cultivated ignorance, its 'learned ignorance', its political indoctrinations, its science perversions, and so on.

It is here, in the domain of cultivated ignorance, where the real 'manmade' danger comes into play.

The near universal refusal by humanity to protect itself

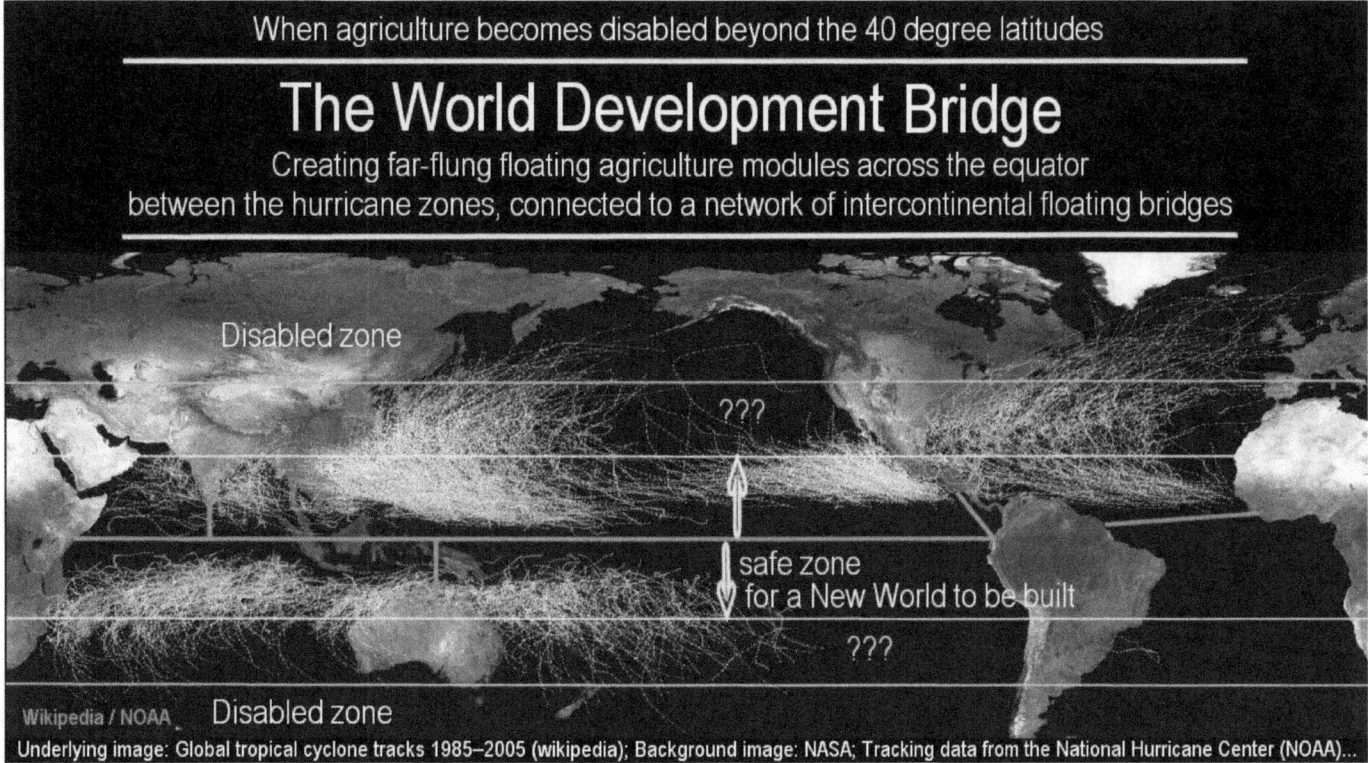

The near universal refusal by humanity to implement a Plan-B option to protect itself against the deep cooling of the Earth that is close at hand, which is as close as the 2050s, is definitely a manmade phenomenon. The refusal by society to be honest with itself about the scientific knowledge it has developed over many years, is not natural for humanity. Humanity is more profound than its current small-minded notions. The ignorance, or learned ignorance, as it was once called, is artificial, and it being artificial, it can be reversed.

Our future is in our hands

Belt and Road Forum 2017 gala

Our future is in our hands. We have the power to create us a grand future with a bright renaissance that far supersedes what the cosmic dynamics impose.

Some day soon, hopefully soon, we may do this and thereby break the ongoing denial of our humanity.

If no Plan-B actions are taken, humanity will be committing suicide

(From the Belt and Road Forum closing gala performance 5/14/2017 Beijing)

If we fail, of course, that is if no Plan-B actions are taken, humanity will be committing suicide by default, almost universally.

Plan-B is big. It is as big as creating a New World

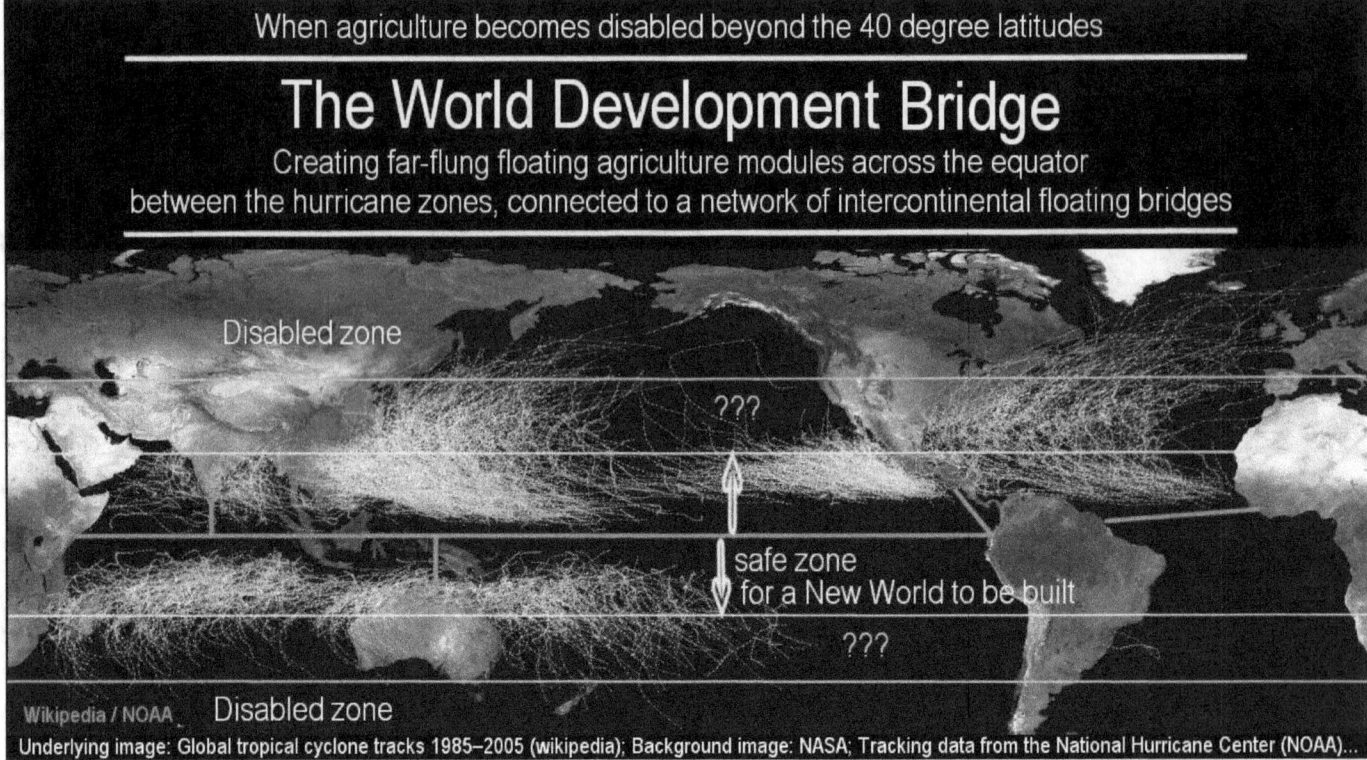

When agriculture becomes disabled beyond the 40 degree latitudes

The World Development Bridge
Creating far-flung floating agriculture modules across the equator
between the hurricane zones, connected to a network of intercontinental floating bridges

Disabled zone

???

safe zone
for a New World to be built

???

Disabled zone

Wikipedia / NOAA

Underlying image: Global tropical cyclone tracks 1985–2005 (wikipedia); Background image: NASA; Tracking data from the National Hurricane Center (NOAA)...

Plan-B is big. It is as big as creating a New World in the tropics that the near Ice Age climate cannot touch. And since there is not enough land in the tropics to accommodate the current world population, the New World needs to be located afloat onto the sea, spanning the oceans along the equator, complete with floating agriculture for 7 billion people, and with thousands of floating cities along the way. That's our option. The technologies, materials, and energy resources exist to implement this option - the only viable option that we have for living in an Ice Age World.

The willingness does not yet exist in humanity

Belt and Road Forum 2017 gala

Only the willingness does not yet exist in humanity to embrace the cosmic reality before it, whereby to write itself a ticket to have a future, and to assure a future for its children.

Since this is the only option we have, and this option is big, as big as creating a new renaissance across the world, it becomes the task of everyone who lives on this planet to assure that the Plan-B implementation will happen.

The largest-ever political transformation of the entire world

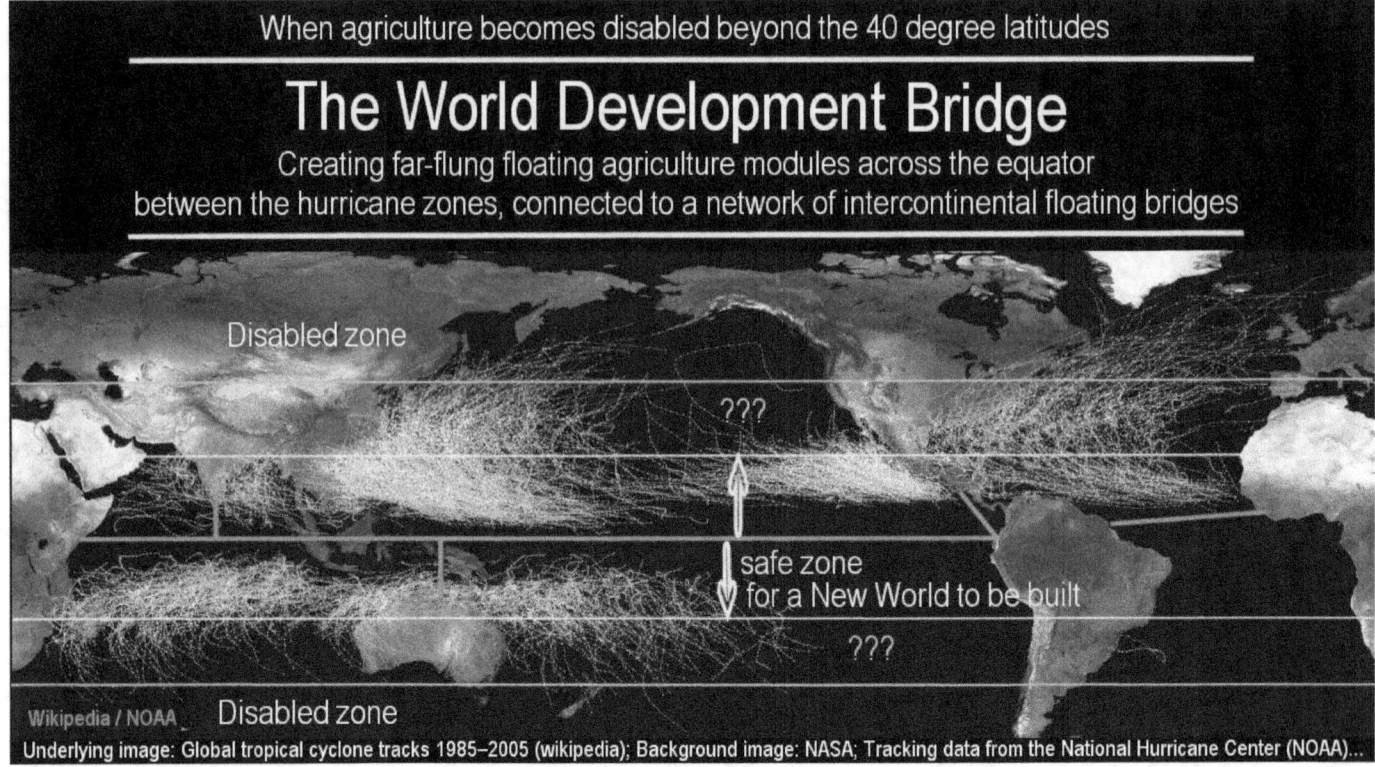

The implementation of Plan-B requires the largest-ever political transformation of the entire world. It requires transformation in economics, industrialization, and in financial architectures.

On this path, when it is chosen, a New Renaissance across the world will be assured, and the future of humanity will be assured with it.

The alternative is unthinkable

From Belt and Road Forum closing gala performance 5/14/2017 Beijing

The alternative is unthinkable. The alternative is suicide. It's as simple as that, and as universal, because no nation on this planet is not affected by the climate collapse that has already begun, that is already causing major crop losses in some parts of the world, and will ultimately trail out into the next Ice Age starting up in the not-so-distant future, potentially in the 2050s.

All nations in the world own the job

BRICS Summit Sept. 2017 Xiamen China - gala performance

This means that all nations in the world own the job to implement Plan-B on a platform of focused universal cooperation and active participation.

Humanity NOT to be committing suicide

This, simply put, is what it means for humanity NOT to be committing suicide.

The BRICS cooperation union

Brazil

Russia

India

China

South Africa

Whether the few tiny footsteps towards universal cooperation, like the BRICS cooperation union will be sufficient as a starting effort, to carry the day, cannot be determined.

The Belt and Road initiative by China

The same can also be said about the Belt and Road initiative by China that is gaining wide acceptance in the world.

The BRICS and Belt and Road appear at the starting gate

BRICS Summit Sept. 2017 Xiamen China - gala performance

While neither of these economic projects are focused on meeting the Ice Age Challenge, a significant effort in the right direction appears to have been made nevertheless. The BRICS and Belt and Road appear to have set the stage at the starting gate. The rest is up to us all. We own the future together, and we own the task to keep our world liveable and grand, no matter how big that task will yet be.

Ultimately, our love for our humanity will carry the day

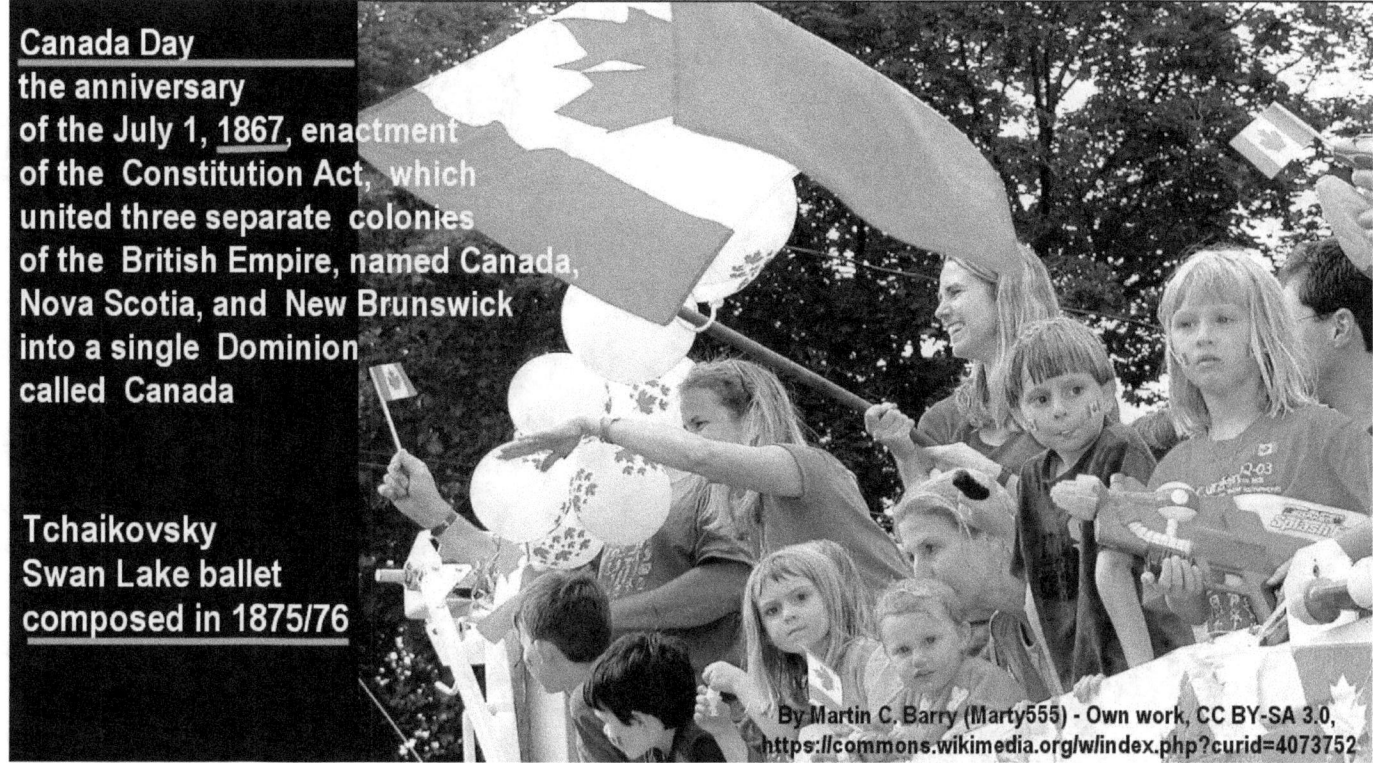

Canada Day
the anniversary
of the July 1, 1867, enactment
of the Constitution Act, which
united three separate colonies
of the British Empire, named Canada,
Nova Scotia, and New Brunswick
into a single Dominion
called Canada

Tchaikovsky
Swan Lake ballet
composed in 1875/76

By Martin C. Barry (Marty555) - Own work, CC BY-SA 3.0,
https://commons.wikimedia.org/w/index.php?curid=4073752

Ultimately, it will be our love for our humanity, and thereby for one another and for our children, which will carry the day.

Whatever politics, institutions, leaders, and cultures reflect

Whatever politics, institutions, leaders, and cultures reflect and promote this fundamental criterion, will flourish by their commitment to it, by which they become drawn into the Plan-B world to secure a viable and bright future for all of humanity.

Those who fail will vanish into oblivion

Those who fail on this count will vanish into oblivion as if they never existed, while those who succeed will prosper in the New Renaissance that their efforts will help bring to fruition by joining hands and hearts across the world.

On this platform of love for our universal humanity unfolding

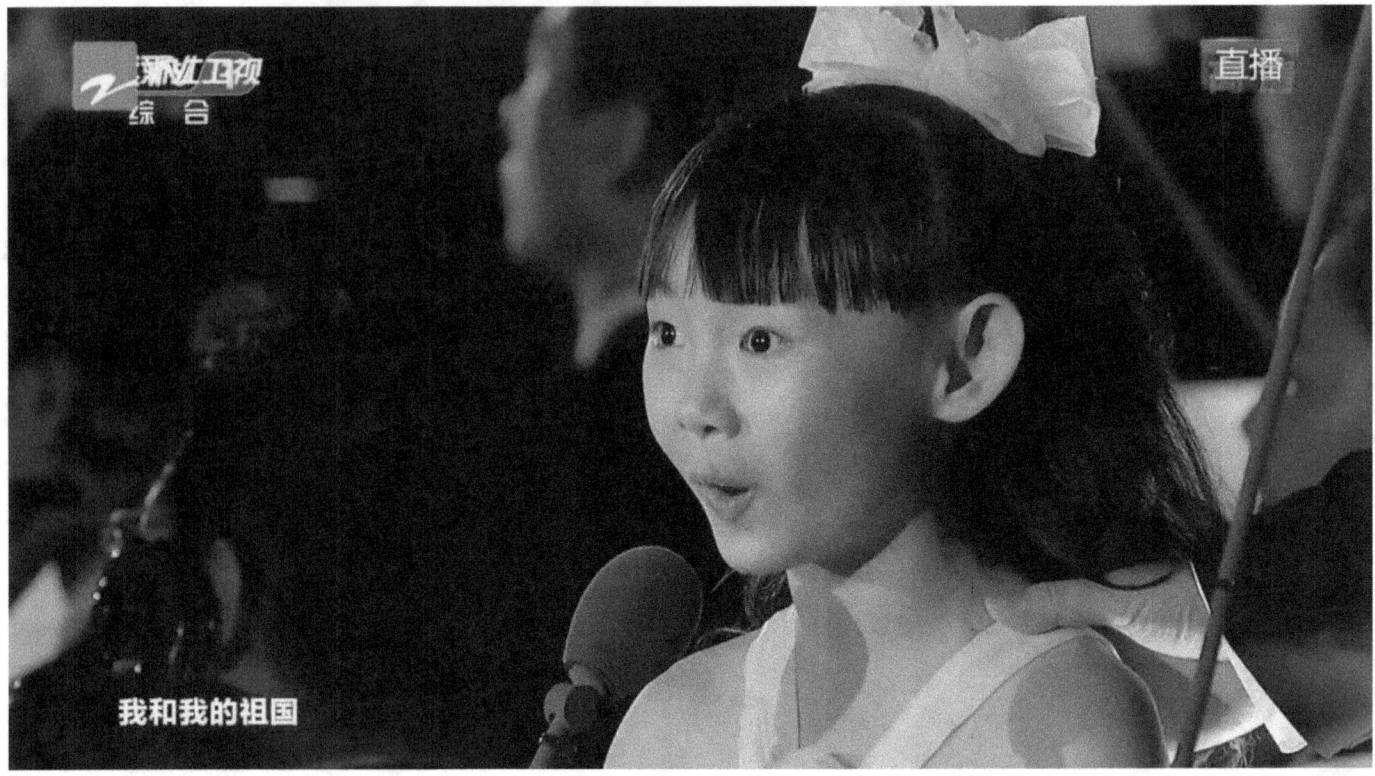

On this basis, on this platform of love for our universal humanity unfolding, I venture to suggest that it becomes actually impossible for a bright New World not to be created on this planet.

That's where we stand today.

More Illustrated Science Books by Rolf A. F. Witzsche

Quick Index to My Books
printed books by Rolf A. F. Witzsche

All Books available from Amazon - follow the links

Ice Age Science - Illustrated New 8.5x11 transcripts (books) from my videos	Ice Age Science - Illustrated Early 6x9 transcripts (books) from my videos
My 14 Novels	My Research Books
Winning Without Victory series New	Kaleidoscope series
Sex and Sacrament series	Christian Science Books

Link to *Cool Science for Kids...* (interactive)

Please Donate - *Home Page*